Managing Your
FAMILY'S
High-Tech Habits

(From Video Games to the Dark Side of the Web)

Managing Your
FAMILY'S
High-Tech Habits

(From Video Games to the Dark Side of the Web)

Arnie Cole
Pam Ovwigho
Michael Ross

An Imprint of Barbour Publishing, Inc.

The authors are represented by and this book is published in association with the literary agency of WordServe Literary Group, Ltd., www.wordserveliterary.com.

Published by goTandem, an imprint of Barbour Publishing, Inc., P.O. Box 719, Uhrichsville, Ohio 44683, www.barbourbooks.com

Our mission is to publish and distribute inspirational products offering exceptional value and biblical encouragement to the masses.

Member of the
Evangelical Christian
Publishers Association

Printed in the United States of America.

Contents

Introduction:
Are We Connected...or Addicted?

*Video Games, Twitter, Smartphones, Instagram:
Everyone Is Riding the Wave of High-Tech Gadgets—
and Sometimes Paying a High Price*

In the last two decades, our society has been transformed by high-tech gadgets, particularly the ubiquitous smartphone and tablet. Most of us carry at least one of these devices with us at all times and in all circumstances. In fact, nine out of ten US adults own a cell phone and 58 percent have a smartphone. Two-fifths of us own a tablet computer.[1]

I (Pam) remember getting my first cell phone before I left home for graduate school. My sole motivation was so that I could call for help if my car broke down. Now I'm one of the majority of Americans who carries a smartphone so that I can stay connected to work, family, and my kids' schools no matter where I am.

Technology touches our lives in so many ways today that it's difficult to remember how things were before. We waited for the weather report on the local news to decide if we needed to carry an umbrella tomorrow. Now we check it instantly on a weather app as we're walking out the door. Staying in touch with family and friends meant phone calls, letters, and even printed pictures sent through the mail. Navigating in a new city required detailed directions and often a map.

As hard as it may be for those of us over thirty to remember that life, it's completely unknown to most millennials. Think about it: a world without smartphones, iPads, and Xboxes is as foreign to our kids as *Little House on the Prairie* is to us!

A few years ago I was talking with Indigo, a young neighbor girl, about her research project on Martin Luther King Jr. She was feeling stressed because her family no longer had Internet access at home and she didn't know how she was going to find the information she needed for her project. When I suggested that she go to the library for some books, she gave me a blank stare. Then when I described how to look up resources and find them in the library, she looked at me as if I had just landed from the planet Pluto and had asked her to take me to her leader.

The truth is Indigo and her generation are "digital natives." As Dr. Archibald Hart and Dr. Sylvia Hart Frejd note in their book *The Digital Invasion*, "The term digital native describes those born after the advent of digital technology. Obviously, they are the younger generation. This group is also referred to as the 'iGeneration' having been born with digital DNA."[2] For Indigo and others of her generation, high-tech gadgets are simply the way things are done.

So if technology gives us all of these good things—staying in touch with loved ones near and far, traveling easier, finding information without a trip to the library, and so on—why a book on managing your high-tech habits? (Actually, if you've picked up this book, we suspect you already know why.)

The Lure of Those Little Blue Screens

In a thought-provoking article on teens and technology, Joanna Moorhead writes:

Teenagers can seem obsessed with their mobile: checking them every few minutes, texting people all the time, checking to see how many "likes" they've got after they've posted on social media, refusing to put their phones to one side when they're sitting 'round the table for Sunday lunch. . . . Then again, that reminds me of some other people I know—me and my husband. We're pretty wedded to our phones as well. Challenge us about it (our teenagers certainly do) and we'll cheerfully reassure you that it's all to do with work, that we're just monitoring some news story, or that we're waiting for an important call. Sadly, though, I have to admit that the reason I check my phone too often is probably for the same reasons my daughters do the same with theirs: boredom and insecurity. Teenagers, of course, have these issues by the bucketload, and I sometimes think mobiles have made adolescents of us all.[3]

Have you noticed? Many of us seem more controlled by our high-tech gadgets than they're controlled by us. A truth we can't escape is that those little electronic devices we love so much can have some pretty nasty side effects. For example. . .

- The temptation to answer every electronic ping has us constantly checking our devices whether we're at work, school, or church or having dinner with friends or watching our child's dance recital. Our divided attention degrades our manners and robs us of true real-life moments.
- Constant connection through emails, texts, and social media leaves us overtaxed with little room for quiet and relaxation. Our minds, bodies, and spirits need rest to function properly. Multiple interruptions each day mean that we expend more energy completing tasks than is really necessary.
- Our social media presence becomes another part

of our identity. We can become obsessed with curating our image on Facebook, Instagram, and Twitter. We start to measure our self-worth by how many friends, followers, and "likes" we have.

- Video and online games and some aspects of social media are so rewarding that we feel compelled to keep playing. Time spent trying to "level up" in the latest game takes away from other activities, including important ones like sleeping, exercising, and spending time with God.

- Pornographic and violent content is just a click away with the endless variety of games, videos, and the Internet. One-fourth of all Internet searches and more than a third of all downloads are pornography-related. Seventy percent of young men (ages eighteen to twenty-four) visit a pornographic website at least once a month.

You may read through this list and think it was written by a bunch of technophobes. That is definitely not the case. Professionally we are part of a ministry that uses media and technology to help people move closer to Jesus on a daily basis. We've spent the past eight years developing goTandem, a customized Bible-engagement and spiritual growth app that meets you at your spiritual level and walks with you daily.

We all rely heavily on our smartphones. We also spend most hours of the workday on a laptop or computer. Arnie's office walls contain multiple screens displaying analytics for our ministry. Mike loves to read on his Kindle and uses many apps, though he still prefers full sentences with proper punctuation and grammar when he's texting. Pam adores the convenience of keeping a family calendar on her phone, texting with her tween daughters, and letting her imagination run wild on Pinterest. Her daughters also attend a 1:1 technology school where every student and every teacher has a device such as a tablet or laptop that they use regularly in class.

In short, we love the convenience and potential of high-tech gadgets. However, we've seen the downside as well. We've had our own struggles with the stress of being constantly connected. Countless times we've found ourselves checking and responding to work emails on weekends, on vacation, and sometimes even in the middle of the night.

We've faced the challenge of parenting tweens who want to spend all of their time playing video games or texting friends instead of playing basketball. In fact, I recently imposed a two-week parent-mandated technology hiatus (aka grounding) on my fourth grader for disobeying our house rules by staying up late playing Minecraft.

We've also heard firsthand from young men, young women, husbands, and wives struggling with pornography addiction. We share some of their stories here, changing the names to protect their identity. Arnie and Mike regularly speak at men's conferences about "Managing the Dark Side of Me." These sessions usually have standing room only, and many men share about their struggles with online porn. Every week we also hear from girlfriends and wives with stories like Anne's:

> *Lately my husband has been relapsing into porn, and although I handle it better than I used to, it still destroys me inside and I feel dead. I am angry at God for not healing my husband's addiction, and for the cycle we go through of me thinking it's all better, and then finding out he's slipping back, and then me feeling dead for a week until numbness takes over again. . . . My husband may have grown and improved, but he is still very much in the struggle, and that affects him, me, our marriage, and everything in between.*

As we look around and see young girls obsessed with Instagram, boys who prefer Xbox to playing in the park, friends staring at iPhones instead of making eye contact, and families like Anne's struggling with pornography addiction, the need for sound guidance on managing our high-tech habits is clear.

Finding Balance *without* Going Off the Grid

For our society as a whole, it's clear that technology is here to stay. Our world has changed and is not going back to the pre-iPhone days. How then do we navigate this high-tech culture in a way that optimizes our health, relationships, and spiritual lives?

Our purpose in writing this book is to give you the information, skills, and tools you need to manage your family's high-tech habits. We've packed these pages full of sound guidance that is grounded in God's Word, based on the latest scientific research, and practical for today's families.

Here's what you'll find in the chapters ahead:

- Chapter 1 begins with some definitions and a self-evaluation quiz. One of the hallmarks of our ministry is meeting people where they are at spiritually. We want to help you and your family where you are at now, and that begins with taking a step back to evaluate your own high-tech habits.

- Chapter 2 dives into the latest neuroscience. Does something as innocent as playing Angry Birds really change our brains? If so, how, and what should we do about it?

- Chapter 3 turns to social science and our own research to see the ups and downs of being socially connected. How do our relationships with our Facebook friends affect our other relationships? We'll navigate our way through this research together, drawing out the most important, practical implications.

- Chapters 4 through 6 focus on managing different aspects of technology, from responding to our phone beeps to managing our video game and social media habits. In each chapter we explore the unique features of technology that can lead us to unhealthy habits and provide tips for how to manage them.

- Chapters 7 and 8 tackle the dark side of the web. The Internet makes pornography anonymously accessible to anyone with just a mouse click or tap on a phone. We'll give you the strategies to protect (or release) your family from this heart-breaking trap.

- Chapter 9 explores how technology is being used to have a spiritual impact. From youth ministry apps to online churches, we'll show you how technology can nurture our faith and spread the Gospel message.

We wrap up the book with a discussion of healthy bound-aries and biblical solutions for a more balanced life. While the Bible doesn't talk about high-tech gadgets specifically, God's Word does contain all we need to live a more bal-anced life and to grow closer to Jesus each day. We'll ex-plore it together and introduce you to a positive app with the right connection.

With this road map in mind, let's begin this journey together!

1

Hashtag Help: Cluing In to Our Electronic Addictions

Definitions and a Self–Evaluation Quiz

Search me, God, and know my heart;
test me and know my anxious thoughts.
PSALM 139:23

Although it seems as though everyone is looking down at a little gadget screen these days, our experiences vary quite a bit. What may be an obsession for one person could be just a minor tool in the life of another. Before diving into our discussion about electronic addictions, consider these true life stories:

Lightning pierces the dark Midwestern sky and thunder shakes the walls of her old farmhouse. Joyce sits straight up in bed, startled awake by the night storm. She rolls over and grabs her phone to see the time. 3:23 a.m. She quickly flips over to her texts to see if there are any tornado warnings. Thankfully there are none. She leans back in the bed, scrolling through the other text messages. She flips to her email and glances through what has come in since she last checked a few hours ago. Pretty much just advertise-ments from her favorite (and not-so-favorite) stores. Noticing her Facebook icon has some notifications, she opens that to browse through her newsfeed. Faith has

completed the '80s rock band quiz and got REO Speed-
wagon. Joyce opens it to see which one she's matched
with. . . . Before she knows it, the clock reads 5:00 a.m.,
little time to sleep before her alarm will sound.

While an Oklahoma couple were busy living out
their fantasies in a video game, police say in real life
their two-year-old daughter was starving to death.
Mark Knapp, 48, and Elizabeth Pester, 33, of Tulsa,
have been arrested and charged with child neglect
and abuse after their young daughter ended up in a
hospital in critical condition. According to the arrest
report obtained by Tulsa World, *the couple's two-*
year-old daughter was rushed to St. Francis Hospital
weighing only 13 lbs. When officers came to take the
parents into custody, they said Knapp and Pester
were busy playing video games.[1]

Have you ever worried that you or someone you love is addicted to their smartphone, iPad, Xbox, or some other electronic gadget? Given the huge role these devices now play in our lives, it's not surprising if you have. In fact, you'd be in good company. Typing the question "Am I addicted to my phone?" into a search engine yields an impressive 15 million hits. These include quizzes and tips from places such as WebMD, wikiHow, CNN, and the Huffington Post.

There's the story of Kevin Holesh, a Pittsburgh-based developer, who developed an app to monitor and set limits on how much time he spends on his iPhone. Kevin noted that he had fallen prey to the endless distractions his phone provided. In a blog post, he describes how evenings spent cooking and walking the dogs with his bride changed: "As we settled in to our new lives together, our evenings got progressively lazier. We'd only take a two-block walk with our dogs and we'd have a movie queued up before we even microwaved leftovers for dinner. We would sign off our work computers at 6pm and immediately wander into the living room and open up our iPhones. Bring on the distractions."[2]

A quick look at the statistics on how we use our devices reveals some trends that are definitely worth noting:

- Industry experts estimate that smartphone users check their phones, on average, 110 to 150 times a day. Over a twelve-hour period, that's about one check every six to seven minutes.[3]
- The majority of us keep our phones within arm's

reach most of the time. Two-thirds of adult smartphone users and 90 percent of teens sleep with or next to their phones.[4]

- We use our phones in some surprising places, including while driving (55 percent), on dinner dates (33 percent), in movie theaters (35 percent), in church (19 percent), and in the shower (12 percent).[5]

- According to author and game developer Jane McGonigal, "We spend 3 billion hours a week as a planet playing videogames. . . . The average young person today in a country with a strong gamer culture will have spent 10,000 hours playing online games by the age of 21. Now 10,000 hours is a really interesting number. For children in the United States 10,080 hours is the exact amount of time you will spend in school from fifth grade to high school graduation if you have perfect attendance."[6]

- Between standard text messaging and "over-the-top" chat/messaging apps, more than 36 billion text messages are sent each day.[7] The average teen sends fifty to sixty messages a day.[8]

- Two out of three Americans have a profile on a

social networking site. Most check social media, particularly Facebook, every day.[9]

The numbers don't lie: technology has become a significant part of our daily lives. And there's a good reason why most of us keep our smartphones with us 24/7—we can accomplish so much with them! There's the practical side: we can check the time, weather, our schedule, our kids' schedules, and checklists and deadlines; we can track our calories eaten and expended, even our blood pressure and heart rate! Then there's the social side: *Did my niece make it to Texas okay? How is Diane celebrating her birthday today? Has Alice gone into labor yet?*

And of course we can't forget the fun side: *Is it my turn in Words with Friends yet? Maybe I can beat that high score in Candy Crush today.*

Yet some are concerned that we're getting too attached to our high-tech gadgets. Reporting on a study of brain scans comparing our minds "on technology" to those of known drug addicts, one journalist writes:

> *The current incarnation of the Internet— portable, social, accelerated, and all pervasive—may be making us not just dumber or lonelier but more*

*depressed and anxious, prone to obsessive compulsive
and attention deficit disorders, even outright psychotic.
Our digitized minds can scan like those of drug
addicts, and normal people are breaking down in sad
and seemingly new ways.*[10]

"There's just something about the medium that's addictive," says Elias Aboujaoude, a psychiatrist at Stanford University School of Medicine, where he directs the Obsessive Compulsive Disorder Clinic and Impulse Control Disorders Clinic. "I've seen plenty of patients who have no history of addictive behavior—or substance abuse of any kind—become addicted via the Internet and these other technologies."[11]

Dr. Peter Whybrow, director of the Semel Institute for Neuroscience and Human Behavior at UCLA and author of The Intuitive Mind: Common Sense for the Common Good, argues that for many people the computer is essentially electronic cocaine. He says, "Our brains are wired for finding immediate reward. With technology, novelty is the reward. You essentially become addicted to novelty."[12]

Although smartphone addiction and video game addiction has become part of mainstream conversation, the professional community of psychologists and psychiatrists is not completely sold on the idea. Curiously, the term "Internet addiction disorder" was first introduced by psychiatrist Ivan Goldberg in 1995 as a spoof on the American Psychological Association's tendency to create a diagnosis for every excessive behavior.[13] He was flabbergasted when several colleagues emailed him to say that they suffer from the disorder and need help.

Does My Health Plan Cover Smartphone Addiction?

In the 2013 update of its *Diagnostic and Statistical Manual*, the manual used by mental health professionals for diagnoses and treatment, the American Psychological Association (APA) did not include Internet addiction, smartphone addiction, or online gaming addiction as a classification. They did, however, include "Internet gaming disorder" as a "condition warranting more clinical research and experience before it might be considered for inclusion in the main book as a formal disorder."[14] The APA's decision largely stems from a lack of empirical evidence about whether this is a definable disorder. Although a number of studies have been published, they generally have design flaws that limit their scientific rigor.

Another main point of contention is whether someone

can actually be addicted to a behavior, as opposed to a substance such as alcohol or cocaine. While the term *addiction* is now commonplace, the scientific definition of addiction has evolved over time, reflecting a deeper understanding of the physical and psychological factors involved. Currently, the American Society of Addiction Medicine provides this definition:

> *Addiction is a primary, chronic disease of brain reward, motivation, memory and related circuitry. Addiction affects neurotransmission and interactions within reward structures of the brain, including the nucleus accumbens, anterior cingulate cortex, basal forebrain, and amygdala, such that motivational hierarchies are altered and addictive behaviors, which may or may not include alcohol and other drug use, supplant healthy, self-care related behaviors. Addiction also affects neurotransmission and interactions between cortical and hippocampal circuits and brain reward structures, such that the memory of previous exposures to rewards (such as food, sex, alcohol and other drugs) leads to a biological and behavioral response to external cues, in turn triggering craving and/or engagement in addictive behaviors. . . The*

frontal cortex of the brain and underlying white matter connections between the frontal cortex and circuits of reward, motivation, and memory are fundamental in the manifestations of altered impulse control, altered judgment, and the dysfunctional pursuit of rewards (which is often experienced by the affected person as a desire to "be normal") seen in addiction—despite cumulative adverse consequences experienced from engagement in substance use and other addictive behaviors.[15]

Let's unpack several features of this definition. First, addiction results from changes in our brain's reward circuitry. God has created us with marvelously intricate and complex bodies and minds, with neural circuits and neurotransmitters that perform a variety of functions in a delicate balance. While many of us realize that our brain chemistry affects our behavior, the reverse is also true: our behavior can affect our brain. We'll talk about this in more detail in the next chapter.

A second key point in the definition is that we become addicted to things that provide us some type of reward or pleasure. Our memories of that pleasure motivate us to seek out whatever caused it more and more.

Repeated exposure changes our brain circuitry, decreasing our ability to resist the temptation and altering our judgment of how much it is really controlling us. Someone who is truly addicted experiences cravings for the reward, must use increasing amounts to feel the same effect, and feels withdrawal symptoms when they don't have it. We are still in the early stages of understanding if and how these things are true when we speak of technology use. However, science has established that interacting with high-tech gadgets does activate the pleasure centers in our brains. Moreover, we crave novelty, something the Internet, online games, and social media excel in providing.

Separating the Evidence from the Hype

As mentioned earlier, the wealth of research conducted today on the topic suffers from a number of problems, including biased samples (for example, large numbers of college students responding to an ad about Internet addiction) and designs that can't tease out cause and effect. The emerging evidence does suggest, however, that there is cause for at least some concern. Anecdotal evidence and some limited surveys suggest that a minority of people develop unhealthy habits related to Internet use, video games, or smartphone usage. Because there is no established definition of Internet addiction or gaming addiction, estimates of how many people are affected range widely. The most reliable US estimates, however, fall into the range of 1.5 percent to 8.9 percent of the population experiencing Internet addiction.[16]

Recent news reports highlight the South Korean government's concerns about Internet addiction among its population. They typically include portraits of young men spending all night at gaming cafés and then popping energy pills as they head to school or work. South Korea has estimated that 2 million of its citizens—roughly 4 percent—are "addicted" to the Internet. With experts disagreeing about whether addiction is even possible, there is of course no standard test or set of criteria for determining if someone has a problem or not. The South Korean government focuses on the amount of time someone spends on their device or playing video games. For example, they classify someone as having a smartphone addiction if they use their device for more than eight hours a day.[17]

Other criteria consider more the consequences of the behavior and how much control the person has over it, rather than simply the amount of time spent in the activity. Researchers ask questions such as how high-tech gadget use is affecting your life and how you feel when you are cut off from your gadgets.

Stepping Back and Looking at the Whole Picture

Based on the criteria utilized in assessing other types of addictions and compulsive behaviors, the APA has developed nine criteria for the proposed Internet gaming disorder:

1. *Preoccupation.* Gaming becomes the main focus of the person's thought life.
2. *Withdrawal.* When forced to stop playing games, restlessness or anxiety ensues.
3. *Tolerance.* The person has to play for longer periods or play more exciting games to experience the same level of pleasure.
4. *Reduce/stop.* Previous attempts to reduce time spent gaming or stopping all together have failed.
5. *Give up other activities.* Interest or participation in other activities has diminished due to gaming.
6. *Continue despite problems.* Gaming continues even when there are negative consequences such as family conflict or falling grades.
7. *Deceive/cover up.* The person lies about or tries to cover up how much he or she is gaming.

8. *Escape adverse moods.* Gaming is regularly used to escape from negative feelings or bad memories.
9. *Risk/lose relationships/opportunities.* Relationships and educational or work opportunities are lost or at risk because of gaming.

While these statements are worded for gaming specifically, we can easily substitute smartphone use or Internet use. Regardless of which specific high-tech habit we're talking about, how much something affects various aspects of your life has a huge influence on whether it's unhealthy. If you're starting to see that you and your spouse argue about how much you're on your phone, it's time to make some changes. If your daughter can't have a face-to-face conversation without checking for a text message and seems anxious when she's not "connected," it's time to help her make some changes. If your son's grades are falling because he's focused on World of Warcraft instead of algebra, it's time to help him put down the controller and take back control of his life.

The following tool is designed to help you evaluate your own high-tech habits. It's not intended as a diagnosis for whether you have an addiction or not. Rather, our goal is to help you reflect on how your use of high-tech gadgets may be affecting different areas of your life.

We've worded the assessment questions so that they focus on smartphone use because it is the most common high-tech gadget stealing our attention these days. However, the same questions apply equally well to iPads, tablets, laptops, Kindle Fires, Wiis, Xboxes, online gaming, and the like.

You can also use this tool as you consider your family's high-tech habits. It can serve as a discussion starter for how you will work together to manage your devices instead of letting your devices manage you.

High-Tech Gadget Use Assessment
Instructions: As you read through the following questions, think about your life over the past month or so. Choose how often each of these statements is true.

	Never	Some-times	Of-ten	Al-ways
My Time				
I spend more time than I planned using my phone.	0	1	2	3

I lose track of time when I'm using my phone.	0	1	2	3
Work Outside or Inside the Home/ Education				
I fall behind on my work because I'm distracted by my phone.	0	1	2	3
Spending time on my phone takes away from the quality of my work.	0	1	2	3
Relationships				
When I'm with others, I have trouble staying focused on our conversation because of my phone.	0	1	2	3
Others complain that I'm using my phone too much.	0	1	2	3
I "hide" behind my phone to avoid difficult conversations or situations.	0	1	2	3
My family relationships are suffering because of my phone use.	0	1	2	3
I spend less time with friends these days because I can just stay up-to-date with them through social media.	0	1	2	3
Spiritual Life				
When I worship, I have trouble staying focused and not turning to my phone.	0	1	2	3
When I'm reading scripture, I have trouble staying focused and not turning to my phone.	0	1	2	3

When I pray, I have trouble staying focused and not turning to my phone.	0	1	2	3
Health				
I spend less time being physically active because I'd rather be on my phone.	0	1	2	3
I'm having some health problems (e.g., headaches, carpal tunnel, weight gain, sleep issues) that are related to how much time I spend on my phone.	0	1	2	3
I check my phone often or text while I drive.	0	1	2	3
I feel very anxious when I'm not able to use my phone as often and when I would like.	0	1	2	3
Total for Each Column				
Your Score—Add the total for each column into one score.				

What Does Your Score Mean?

As we mentioned earlier, our High-Tech Gadget Use Assessment is designed to help you reflect on your own high-tech habits and how they are impacting your life. The higher your score on this tool, the more changes you need to make so that those habits are healthier. Generally, this is what your score means:

If your score is less than 16...

Congratulations! It sounds like you have a healthy relationship with your high-tech gadgets. Hopefully you've passed that on to your family as well. The remainder of the book is full of information and tips that can keep your tech habits strong and healthy.

If your score is between 16 and 29...

While you may not think of yourself as a "smartphone addict," you've developed some unhealthy tech habits. You're probably starting to feel the not-so-pleasant side effects and hear complaints from loved ones. The good news is that the strategies outlined in this book will help you rid your life of those unhealthy habits and avoid developing any more.

If your score is 30 or more...

Your high-tech habits are having a big impact on your life. You have probably already seen the effects, especially on your relationships. Please know that there is hope. Today you can start making changes that will free you from that little screen and help you take back your real life.

2

What Happens in Our Brains

Neurotransmitters, Multitasking, and Blue Lights

*The truth is that everything you do changes your brain.
Everything. Every little thought or experience plays a role in
the constant wiring and rewiring of your neural networks.
So there is no escape. Yes, the Internet is rewiring your brain.
But so is watching television. And having a cup of tea. Or not
having a cup of tea. Or thinking about the washing on Tues-
days. Your life, however you live it, leaves traces in the brain.*
TOM STAFFORD, BBC

When I look at the human brain, I'm still in awe of it.
DR. BENJAMIN CARSON[1]

*Do not conform to the pattern of this world,
but be transformed by the renewing of your mind.
Then you will be able to test and approve what
God's will is—his good, pleasing and perfect will.*
ROMANS 12:2

Hidden in its fortress of bone lies the brain, the nerve
and command center of the human body. Although this
wonderfully complex organ plays a role in every single
thought, emotion, and experience, it remains quietly in
the background, with few of us ever giving it a thought
(yes, pun intended).

But how the brain works and how technology can affect those workings are a central concern for those advocating warning about too much high-tech gadget use. Scientists used to view the brain as an unchangeable organ with a structure that was fairly set after childhood and had no way to regenerate cells when cells died. Today we know that the brain is, in fact, always changing. Each day the hippocampus, a part of our brain involved in learning and memory, forms new cells. Connections among the brain's 100 billion nerve cells develop or are altered as we interact with the world. This neuroplasticity, or ability of our brains to change, is necessary for learning and creating new memories. It also helps us to recover from brain injury by allowing for a specific body or brain functionality to "move" to a different region of the brain if and when necessary.

So basic neuroscience then would lead us to conclude that the warning that technology is "rewiring" our brains is on some level correct. Basically everything we do—from reading a book to riding a horse to enjoying a hot cup of cocoa on a cold winter night—rewires our brains. We need to move beyond this basic fact to understand what types of changes are occurring and what the consequences of those changes are.

Hypotheticals from a Young Science

Consider studies by UCLA neuroscientist Dr. Gary Small. He conducted brain scans of experienced and novice Internet users while they were performing basic Internet searches. Both groups, all between the ages of fifty-five and seventy-eight, showed activation in the language, reading, memory, and visual abilities regions; however, the experienced Internet users also showed activity in areas known for working memory and decision making. Participants were then asked to conduct Internet searches at home for one hour a day over seven days.

The second scan revealed that the novices showed the same activation patterns as the experienced Internet users. In addition to showing how our high-tech habits can change brain functioning, the results also suggest that they can be used to enhance cognitive functioning in older adults.[2]

Interesting Brain Facts

- Certain areas of our brain may become larger or more active if we "specialize" in something. Professional cab drivers have more activity in the area involved with spatial relationships than people who don't navigate for a living. The difference is bigger for cab drivers than for bus drivers who follow an established route.[*]

- Neurons make up 10 percent of our brains. The other 90 percent are glia cells that hold it all together. (This is why some say that we use only 10 percent of our brains.)[†]

- Although the brain makes up only 2 percent of your body mass, it hogs 20 percent of your oxygen and 20 percent of your sugar.[‡]

- Smartphone users' brains have an enhanced representation of their thumbs. According to a study published in the *Journal of Current Biology*, the more they text, the larger the representation.[§]

---

[*]Eleanor A. Maguire, Katherine Woollett, Hugo J. Spiers, "London Taxi Drivers and Bus Drivers: A Structural MRI and Neuropsychological Analysis," *Hippocampus*, 2006, 1091–1101.

[†]"Myth—You Only Use 10 Percent of Your Brain," BrainFacts.org, 2011, http://www.brainfacts.org/sensing-thinking-behaving/awareness-and-attention/articles/2011/10-percent-myth/.

[‡]"Human Brain Statistics," StatisticsBrain.com, March 12, 2014, http://www.statistic-brain.com/human-brain-statistics/.

[§]Anne-Dominique Gindrat, Magali Chytiris, Myriam Balema, Eric M. Rouiller, Arko Ghosh, "Use-Dependent Cortical Processing from Fingertips in Touchscreen Phone Users," *Journal of Current Biology*, January 2015, 109–16.

This benefit has some potential downsides as well. One of those is that the brain may lose some functions that are no longer deemed necessary as it is building new ones. For example, while we may become experts in scanning for information on a web page, our ability to read print for extended periods of time may suffer. Texting may help us stay in touch with more people more frequently but may degrade our spelling skills and our ability to have a genuine face-to-face conversation.

We're already seeing signs of this downside in the controversy over handwriting. The 2013 Common Core Standards for Education include learning how to type on a keyboard and print by hand but not how to write in cursive. Some applaud the change, saying that cursive writing has no place in our type-focused society. Still, some states, such as Indiana, have chosen to keep cursive writing in their curriculum, saying that kids need to be able to read cursive writing on things such as greeting cards, teachers' assignments and feedback, and the US Constitution.

This is just one of many current controversies, and many more are likely to come. Each day it seems a new book warns of the dangers of technology use, Internet and online gaming addiction, and other high-tech habits.

Yet many of these concerns remain largely "What ifs?" at this time. Educators, psychologists, and neurologists are conducting more and more studies each day, furthering our understanding of how our minds and behaviors are developing, changing, and adapting as technology becomes more ingrained in our lives.

With the emerging research in mind, we'll tread lightly in this chapter. Rather than going down the long trail of "what ifs," we'll stick close to the empirical evidence. We'll explore four topics that represent the most common concerns:

1. Our brains find high-tech gadgets rewarding, and that can be too much of a good thing.
2. Our brains hate to be bored and find high-tech gadgets exciting, but they still need periods of rest.
3. High-tech gadgets encourage us to multitask, but this isn't consistent with the way our brains work.
4. Light from high-tech screens disrupts our natural sleep cycles.

We end the chapter with a discussion of how we all can develop high-tech habits that will keep our minds healthy.

Concern #1: Our brains find high-tech gadgets rewarding, and that can be too much of a good thing.

Think about the last time you checked your smartphone for messages or logged into your Facebook account. What were you seeking? The specifics may vary—looking for a text confirming that your flight is on time, seeing if the photos from Saturday's banquet are posted, and so on—but your brain sees only one thing: "reward." Our minds crave novelty and our high-tech gadgets give us "new information" in spades. Just as the dog on the Beggin' Strips commercial will do anything for "BACON!" your brain wants "NOVELTY!"

Neuroscience reveals that high-tech activities such as playing online games do indeed activate our brain's reward system.[3] This causes a release of the neurotransmitter dopamine. We experience this as a feeling of pleasure and happiness.

Activating this system too often can cause problems though. It can result in "dopamine flooding" and the loss of that pleasurable feeling. Dopamine flooding is implicated in addiction to substances such as alcohol and cocaine. When the system is excessively activated, pleasure starts to diminish. In order to get those rewards back, the addict starts using more.

To deepen our understanding of this process and the concern that we can become too dependent on our high-tech gadgets, let's think about this in terms of behavior modification. I (Arnie) am a behaviorist by training and have spent most of my career developing methodologies, processes, and best practices to instill significant behavioral change in individuals with severe disabilities and violent behaviors. One of the things that fascinates me about high-tech gadgets in general—and gaming in particular—is that they are perfectly designed to get us to want more.

Let's go back to the original behaviorists Pavlov and Skinner. Imagine that you want to train your dog Max to ring the doorbell. (One of us [Pam] actually had a family member try to train her dog to do this, though she didn't use the approach we're outlining here.)

Max loves bacon-flavored dog treats. So you decide you will give Max a dog treat when he successfully rings the doorbell. Now you have to decide how often you will give Max the treat. You can do it every time he rings the doorbell or every third time, or you can mix it up—sometimes giving him a treat and sometimes not.

Which schedule do you think will maximize Max's motivation to ring the doorbell? If you said the last one, *the random reward schedule*, you are correct. Random rewards are powerful stuff. They are what keep gamblers at the slot machines, why inconsistent parenting produces whiny children, and why Max will keep ringing that doorbell long after you want him to stop. Because the reward comes randomly when we engage a certain behavior, we keep doing it in the hope that this time we will get the reward.

And in case you haven't already guessed, this is why many of us find ourselves mindlessly swiping our phones, looking for the next text message, email, or social media notification. Sometimes we get the reward—a new text message, email, or notification—the novelty our brains love.

As we discussed earlier, science has yet to establish whether we can truly become addicted to high-tech gadgets. However, we may find that we have developed some bad habits such as continuously checking our phone. Later chapters give many tips and strategies for changing those habits. In the meantime, it's helpful to understand how habits may have developed. We can, at a minimum, become more attuned to our own behavior. Next time you find yourself mindlessly reaching for your phone, stop and ask yourself, *Why? Why do I want to do that now?*

Concern #2: Our brains hate to be bored and find high-tech gadgets exciting, but they still need periods of rest.

How online gaming in particular affects the brain is another area that scientists are exploring. These virtual worlds give us battles to fight, treasure to find, empires to build, and pets to rescue. When you're playing one of these games, you can feel the excitement rise and your heart racing as you try to beat the clock and get to the next level.

When we experience excitement or stress, our brain releases the neurotransmitter cortisol. This occurs whether we're feeling the thrill of running from a Creeper in Minecraft or narrowly missing a collision with a semi in real life. Cortisol's job is to calm us down by activating our brain's tranquilizer receptors. That is, it's supposed to be the signal to release the neurotransmitters that dial back our heartbeat and restore inner peace.

Similar to what we see with dopamine, flooding our system with cortisol causes problems. Too much and the tranquilizer receptors get overwhelmed, making it difficult to calm down and rest. Our Creator has not designed us to go at full tilt, 100 mph, with all of the subsequent physical consequences all of the time. Rather, we need periods of rest.

Our brains at rest are a marvelous thing. When we are concentrating on a task, activity (measured as blood flow and how oxygenated the blood is in that region) decreases in certain brain regions, including the hippocampus and medial prefrontal cortex. These regions are implicated in a variety of cognitive functions, including long-term memory, spatial navigation, complex cognitive behavior planning, decision making, and social behavior moderation. Brain scans show that when we are idle, at rest, or daydreaming, the activity in these regions increases.[4]

Is our high-tech world really starting to rob us of the ability to experience quiet and stillness? Consider a fascinating series of studies by researchers at the University of Virginia. They had college-student participants spend six to fifteen minutes by themselves in an unadorned room. Participants were not allowed to have any of their belongings in the room—no books, no phones, no pens. They were told to entertain themselves with their thoughts, remaining in their seats and staying awake. Before reading on to what the researchers found, take a moment and imagine participating in this experiment yourself. How would you feel?

The participants in the studies did not enjoy this time

alone with their thoughts and noticed that their minds wandered a lot. Later studies with community participants and people from a local church showed similar results.

Many participants found being alone with their thoughts so unpleasant that they preferred to administer electric shocks to themselves. Of the people who had earlier said they would *pay* to avoid an electric shock, two-thirds of males (ages twelve to eighteen) and 25 percent of females gave themselves at least one during the "thinking" period.[5]

Consider what these findings imply for our spiritual lives. If we can't sit alone with our thoughts for a few minutes, how can we be still before our God?

Center for Bible Engagement research shows that we thrive spiritually when we engage with God's Word most days of the week. Engaging scripture means:

- *receiving* the words of scripture in our minds through reading or listening to the Bible,

-

- *reflecting* on the meaning of God's Word in our minds and hearts, and

- *responding* to God by applying His Word to our lives.

All three of these aspects are critical. If we just receive the Word without reflecting on it, we end up with head knowledge without heart knowledge. The constant stimulation from high-tech gadgets may keep us from really quieting our minds and spending time meditating on how God is speaking into our lives.

Concern #3: High-tech gadgets encourage us to multitask, but this isn't consistent with the way our brains work.

A third concern related to high-tech gadgets centers on their "encouragement" to multitask and our limited ability to attend to more than one thing at a time. Our brains are complex with enormous processing power. As physicist Michio Kaku states, "There are an estimated 100 billion neurons residing inside the skull with an exceptional amount of neural connections and pathways."[6]

Ultimately, however, our minds optimally focus on one task at a time. We can certainly perform many tasks in rapid-fire sequence—just watch a parent who is helping one child with homework, while also preparing dinner and caring for a baby. When we try to do two tasks that require focused attention at the same time, one will inevitably suffer.[7]

Although we may tell ourselves we are doing two things at the same time, the truth is that we're asking our brain to switch between the tasks. Each time we switch, we disrupt the flow of the task. When we return to it, we have to reorient ourselves back to where we were. These switches or disruptions ultimately degrade how well we perform the task.

These are tough truths, because multitasking has become a big part of our daily lives. We can almost hear the protests as we write this: "That may be true of most people, but I'm really good at it." Or "Well, some tasks, like meetings, only require part of my attention." The truth is we've said them to ourselves as well. The neuroscience data tell us otherwise.

We also see the consequences of divided attention around us. We see the tragic accidents caused by someone texting while driving. We hear the lapses in conversations when one person chooses to check her phone while having coffee with a friend.

Concern #4: Light from high-tech screens disrupts our natural sleep cycles.

Each of us has a circadian rhythm—a set of physical, mental, and behavioral changes that follow a roughly twenty-four-hour cycle. Circadian rhythms are critical in determining sleep patterns. Your body naturally follows this cycle, although environmental factors can affect it as well. Anyone who has ever suffered from jet lag knows what it's like when this cycle (especially as it relates to sleep) is thrown off.

Scientists have known for years that light can affect

our sleep by preventing the release of melatonin, a natural chemical that calms our bodies down to prepare for sleep. Recent studies show that the blue light emitted from electronic screens suppresses melatonin more than other types of light.[8] The bad news for those of us who like to read a little on our e-reader or play one last game of Solitaire before bed is that doing so can make it harder to fall asleep.

Generally, physicians recommend that we get seven to nine hours sleep a night, with children and teenagers needing a bit more. The negative consequences of sleep deprivation on our thinking, emotions, and even physical health are well documented. Not getting enough sleep leaves us vulnerable to nodding off while driving or having difficulty performing our daily tasks. Insufficient sleep is associated with chronic diseases such as hypertension, diabetes, depression, and obesity.

The Centers for Disease Control (CDC) are so concerned about Americans' poor sleep habits that they've declared insufficient sleep a public health epidemic. If our high-tech habits are interfering with healthy sleep habits, we need to make some changes. CDC data reveal that more than one-third of adults typically get less than seven hours of sleep a day and 38 percent accidentally fell asleep during the day at least once in the past month. Each year drowsy driving causes about 1,550 traffic fatalities and 40,000 injuries. Among high school students, who need nine to ten hours of sleep, only three out of ten get at least eight hours of sleep a night.[9]

Of course, many factors, such as packed schedules, health problems, and poor sleep habits, contribute to making us a drowsy nation. Some of these things we can change and some we can't. Too much time on our high-tech devices at night can definitely be one of the change-able factors, especially for teens. Recent media reports have noted the social media trend of teens posting pic-tures of themselves staying up until the wee hours of the morning. The pictures are tagged with hashtags such as #vamping[10] (referring to the popularity of vampire series such as *Twilight*), #breakingnight, and #notsleepingatall.

One easy change, strongly recommended by the American Academy of Pediatrics, is to remove screens from our bedrooms at night. For young children, this means no computers, televisions, iPads, or other elec-tronics in their bedrooms at all. Teens and adults should impose a nightly curfew, when all high-tech gadgets get stored in a common place until morning.

Healthy High-Tech Habits, Healthy Life

How can knowing these "brain risks" help you and your family manage your high-tech habits? First, you now know the signs to look for that will warn you when your technology use has become unhealthy. These signs include:

- Spending more and more time on your high-tech gadget in order to feel the same amount of enjoyment.
- Having trouble concentrating when you are focusing on an activity or trying to meditate on a topic.
- Performing tasks poorly because you are multi-tasking instead of focusing on one task at a time.
- Feeling drowsy and sleep-deprived because you are using your high-tech gadget at night and having trouble falling asleep.

You can avoid the brain risks by adopting healthy habits such as the following:

- *When possible, set a time limit for how long you will use your gadget.* For example, I (Pam) love the Bejeweled Blitz game on my phone and *really* want to beat my high score. But to keep myself from staying up too late playing, I make a three-game rule for myself—three games and it gets turned off.

- *Practice spending a few minutes each day sitting quietly before the Lord.* Use this time to meditate on a particular scripture verse and talk to your Father. Don't be too hard on yourself at first if you find this tough. With practice you will find you can sit for longer and longer periods.

- *Evaluate your tendencies to multitask.* Take a good hard look at how these may be affecting your performance.

- *Stop trying to multitask in situations that require your full attention.* When you are driving, staying off your phone is imperative. If texting while driving is a strong temptation for you, put your phone in another part of the car where you can't reach it from the driver's seat.

- *Discuss with your family the need for good sleep habits.* Adequate rest plays a key role in brain development and health. Track your sleep every day for a week to see if your schedule and routines are allowing you to get adequate rest.

- *Establish family rules that promote healthy sleep.* Consider eliminating screens (TVs, game consoles, computers, laptops, etc.) from bedrooms and having a curfew for turning in portable devices in the evening.

3

Virtual vs. Real Relationships

*The Rise of "Connected Isolation"
and Other Modern Problems*

I feel like everyone always has a phone in their hand, checking it constantly. It puts a damper on conversation when the person you're talking to is constantly checking their phone or device—I know I'm guilty of it!

LYDIA

Technology can make us too connected. You really see every little thought of some people, and it can really harm a relationship. Mostly, I think some people don't think before they tweet or post.

ANNA

A friend loves at all times, and a brother is born for a time of adversity.

PROVERBS 17:17

Recently we surveyed teens and young adults about how technology affects their relationships. They nearly universally responded that it helps them communicate faster and more often. They can stay in touch with friends and family better across the miles.

These tools increase the volume of communication and the type. Yet, as the quotes above illustrate, they also were very aware of how technology can hurt their relationships. Reading someone's Facebook posts can create a false sense of intimacy because we know the facts of an event and maybe some of the emotions our friend is experiencing as well. Still, we're missing the nonverbal cues like tone of voice and facial expressions that give communication its richness and depth.

Face-to-face interactions take time, effort, and energy—three resources often in short supply in our fast-paced, connected world. It's not surprising then that we're often tempted to be lazy with our relationships. The convenience of sharing news or checking in with friends via text messages, chat, or a social media post seems like a better choice than spending time together in person. Doing this once or twice over the course of a long-term relationship is probably not a big deal. However, too much and there's the potential for the relationship to deteriorate.

Our high-tech habits can be hazardous to our relationships in four other ways as well:

- *Risk #1: Connected isolation.* High-tech gadgets are great at distracting us, especially from spending quality time with our families and friends. During the day, kids are in school and parents are either at work or at home. Evenings are often packed with lessons, sports, meetings, and home-work. When we have a free hour in the rush of it all, we are tempted to unwind by turning on the TV, computer, or game console. But when we do this we can miss out on connecting with one another.

- *Risk #2: Hiding behind the screen.* No one likes having tough conversations or dealing with emotionally charged, difficult situations. Instead of pushing through discomfort, it's tempting to retreat behind a high-tech screen. Another form of hiding is to allow the screen to be a mask, leading you to do and say things online that you would not do in real life.

- *Risk #3: Getting the message but not the meaning.* When we rely too much on high-tech gadgets for communicating, we risk being misunderstood and misunderstanding others. There's a saying that 90 percent of communication is nonverbal. While this much-touted figure is somewhat of an urban myth, the truth is that text messages, emails, and phone calls are not nearly as information rich as talking face-to-face. Trying to convey our messages in 140 characters or less without the benefit of tone of voice, body language, and facial expressions can result in miscommunication and hurt feelings.

- *Risk #4: Opening the door to temptation.* Social media and the Internet can bring temptations to reconnect with old flames, to cheat on our spouses, and to view pornography into our homes. If we don't proactively take steps to guard our marriages, our high-tech habits can lead to mistrust, jealousy, and betrayal.

God created us to be relational, and living a healthy life means having healthy relationships. Let's explore these four areas where our high-tech habits can put our relationships at risk.

Risk #1: Connected isolation

As we instant-message, e-mail, and text, technology redraws the boundaries between intimacy and solitude. . . . After an evening of avatar-to avatar talk in a networked game, we feel, at one moment, in possession of a full social life and, in the next, curiously isolated, in tenuous complicity with strangers. We build a following on Facebook and Twitter and wonder to what degree our followers are friends. We recreate ourselves as online personae and give ourselves new bodies, homes, jobs, and romances. Yet, suddenly, in the half-light of virtual community, we may feel utterly alone. As we distribute ourselves, we may abandon ourselves. Sometimes people experience no sense of having communicated after hours of connection. And they report feelings of closeness when they are paying little attention. In all of this, there is a nagging question: Does virtual intimacy degrade our experience of the other kind and, indeed, of all encounters, of any kind?[1]

In her book *Alone Together*, psychologist and Massachusetts Institute of Technology professor Sherry Turkle explores how robots and our use of high-tech communication may be changing how we relate with each other. She points out that a review of seventy-two studies conducted between 1979 and 2009 shows that college students today have less empathy than college students thirty years ago. Based on her own interviews with 300 children and 150 adults, Turkle argues that people who choose to spend much of their time connecting online are more isolated in their real lives, emotionally disconnected, mentally fatigued, and anxious.[2]

Others have expressed similar concerns that we're becoming lonelier as we replace personal interaction with virtual interaction. Their conclusions arise from two different lines of research, each with their own strengths and weaknesses. First, some longitudinal studies, such as the 2010 AARP survey, found that 35 percent of adults over age forty-five experience chronic loneliness.[3] Just a decade earlier that rate had been 20 percent. Although the AARP study did not find differences in technology use between lonely older adults and those who were not lonely, other studies have found a relationship. This second line of research typically looks at the correlation between loneliness and social media use. Most find that high social media involvement relates to more loneliness.

So is Facebook making you lonely? Unfortunately, the empirical evidence is not that clear. It could be, as many warn, that spending a lot of time online or engaged in virtual worlds makes people more isolated and lonely. However, an equally valid explanation is that people who are isolated and lonely to begin with turn more to the online world, looking for the social connection they are craving.

Several studies add credibility to the second explanation. A massive study of 180,000 Facebook users revealed associations between certain personality traits, such as extraversion and neuroticism, and social media activity. The authors note, "One possible explanation for the correlation between neuroticism scores and the number of likes and groups is that more neurotic users often tend to feel negative emotions such as anxiety, anger, or depression. One way to help alleviate these is to seek support from friends. Thus neurotic users may seek support through activity in Facebook groups or hope to get support by liking other users' updates, hoping they would reciprocate by supporting them."[4]

How social media affects you, then, could depend on where you are starting in terms of your personality, your emotions, and how you generally interact with other people. If you use Facebook, for example, to interact with friends by liking and commenting on their posts, you will likely feel more connection and the friendship will develop. This type of personalized communication more resembles an in-person interaction and thus leaves us feeling more satisfied and less lonely.[5]

On the other hand, simply "consuming" social media by browsing through a newsfeed or updating your own status can leave you feeling down. We love to compare ourselves to one another. Using social media in a non-personal way seems to feed our natural critics:

"Oh, I see little Margo's soccer team won the tournament. If only my Zoe didn't have two left feet."

"The Andersons finished their kitchen remodel. Didn't they just start two weeks ago? Ugh! When is Tony going to finish painting our cabinets?"

"Bethany, Leah and Renee were all tagged in that photo at the game. And here I sit alone on another Saturday night. Must be nice to be invited places."

Do any of these sound familiar to you? Maybe you've said them to yourself.

Although scientists are just now beginning to tease apart the connected isolation puzzle, it's not too early for you to examine your own life. Are you feeling isolated and lonely? Look at how much you are interacting with people in real life and online. Have you fallen into some lazy habits and stopped making the effort to spend time with family and friends? Are you consuming social media more than participating? If so, challenge yourself to make some changes.

Risk #2: Hiding behind the screen

Think about the last time you had to have a difficult conversation with someone, to share some news or decision that you knew would upset them. How did you convey the message? Are you happy with the way you handled it? Do you wish you had handled it differently?

When we're dealing with opposing points of view, the end of a relationship, anger, betrayal, or any painful topic, we may be tempted to avoid the discomfort of dealing with it face-to-face. Real-life, in-person conversations open the door to answering awkward questions, seeing the hurt or disappointment in the other person's eyes, and letting them see us cry. Why not use our high-tech gadget to send the message and avoid all of that?

One reason is discussed more in the next section: text-only forms of communication deprive us of nonverbal cues, leading to misunderstanding and making a bad situation worse.

Another reason to save difficult conversations for face-to-face meetings is that the cold nature of a text message, email, or social media post compounds the pain of the message itself. We've all been in those situations where someone has betrayed us or hurt us so deeply that we just want them out of our lives. In our anger we want the breakup to be as painful as possible for the one who hurt us.

Christ calls us, however, to respond like Him, not the world (see, for example, Matthew 7:12). Jesus calls us to face the difficult task of working toward healing and forgiveness. Of course, if the other person is a physical threat to you, a face-to-face conversation may not be possible or advisable.[6] Outside of these situations though, a real-life discussion gives both parties more healing and closure.

For many of us, screens become masks in social interactions. We fire off a hotly worded email or text in the flush of anger or pain without considering the long-term relational consequences. We make social media comments that are funny to us or make us look smart but deeply cut the person on the receiving end.

A recent study from the Pew Research Internet project reveals these startling statistics:
- Three-fourths of adult Internet users have

witnessed someone being harassed online; 40 percent have personally experienced it.

- Using offensive names and purposefully embarrassing someone represent the most common forms of harassment.

- A quarter have seen someone being physically threatened.

- One out of five has witnessed online sexual harassment.[7]

As representatives of God's love on earth, we must carefully consider all of our communication—electronic or otherwise. A wise mentor once advised me (Pam) never to write anything in an email that I wouldn't be comfortable seeing on the front page of the *Baltimore Sun* newspaper. I strive to apply this wise advice to all of my communication, whether a phone call, email, text, letter, website comment, or something else.

Young people often find it more difficult to deal with painful emotions and have less experience with relationships in general. As parents, teachers, and mentors, we are responsible to help them navigate the world of high-tech communication. The good news is that more and more schools are helping in these efforts with curriculum that addresses relationships, communication, and online bullying in particular.

We will circle back to this issue again in chapters 4 through 6. In the meantime, we want to leave you with some tips. When you find yourself tempted to hide behind your high-tech gadget, it's important to stop and acknowledge why you feel that way. Take time to think through what the consequences will be if you give in to that temptation. Spend some time in prayer about the situation and how you should respond.

Risk #3: Getting the message but not the meaning

Each day we communicate through a host of mediums: text messages, email, social media posts, phone calls, written letters, and face-to-face conversations. Some of this communication is mundane or just facts: what time the meeting starts, how much the water bill is, and whether your son remembered to put the trash out. Other is more personal, sensitive, intimate, or complex. Matching the content of the message with the medium for conveying it is key to successful communication.

According to media richness theory, richer communication mediums are more effective than less rich mediums. Pure text forms (for example, letters, emails, and text messages) are less rich, lacking many of the nonverbal cues we rely on to convey and understand deeper meaning. These forms, then, are best for simple, straightforward messages.

Phone calls are a bit richer, allowing us to hear the other person's voice. But face-to-face conversations provide the richest and most effective communication. Talking with another in person affords us the luxury of using all nonverbal cues (well, except emojis!). We can hear their tone of voice and see their body language and facial expressions. As we talk back and forth, we can respond to each other's words and nonverbal cues.

Perhaps you've seen the images of funny text message failures floating around the Internet. Maybe you've experienced some not-so-funny ones in real life yourself. We have—times when an email is misunderstood, a text message is too clipped, and someone's feelings get hurt. Often repairing the relationship requires switching to a richer form of communication such as a phone call or, ideally, a face-to-face conversation.

Avoiding these types of misunderstandings requires matching the message with the medium. Email, text messages, and other entirely verbal forms work best for communicating facts. Topics that are more complex or emotional are best saved for the richer communication mediums of video conferencing and in-person discussions.

Risk #4: Opening up the door to temptation

The accessibility of the Internet opens doors to vast stores of information like nothing before. But with the good there is also the bad: this accessibility, combined with anonymity and affordability, brings the temptation of online infidelity into our homes.

These days it's easy to find and reconnect with an old flame online. An innocent curiosity about where they are now and how they are doing can lead to frequent email, text, or social media conversations. The evil beauty is that these connections are free of the day-to-day grind that weighs on marriages, such as bills, house repairs, packed schedules, and sick kids.

Relationship experts are still struggling to define what constitutes online infidelity. Is infidelity limited to actual physical contact? What about cybersex and emotional infidelity? The emerging evidence suggests that all of these forms are equally damaging to the offended spouse. Moreover, even innocent connections with someone of the opposite sex may damage the trust between spouses.[8]

As we'll discuss more in chapters 7 and 8, affairs aren't the only relationship threat from high-tech devices.

The saturation of pornographic content on the Internet endangers children, men, women, and marriages.

Sidestepping High-Tech Relationship Hazards

Covering all of the potential relationship risks that may be associated with our fascination with high-tech gadgets in one chapter is impossible. The four risks we discussed, however, are the major ones that psychologists and relationship experts are concerned about.

We close by encouraging you to consider your own high-tech use and relationships. Identify those areas where you may need to adopt new high-tech habits to make your relationships thrive. Are you or someone you love isolated behind a screen? Are you using your gadgets to avoid facing tough problems, conversations, and decisions? How carefully do you consider the messages you send and how they are received?

Once you've answered these questions, use some of the strategies in this book to make changes. Your relationships will thank you.

4

Managing Our Addiction to Devices

When Your Cell Phone Beeps, You Don't Have to Jump

I am not being flippant when I say that all of us suffer from addiction. Nor am I reducing the meaning of addiction. I mean in all truth that the psychological, neurological, and spiritual dynamics of full-fledged addiction are actively at work in every human being. The same processes that are responsible for addiction to alcohol and narcotics are also responsible for addiction to ideas, work, relationships, power, moods, fantasies, and an endless variety of other things. We are all addicts in every sense of the word.

GERALD G. MAY, MD[1]

Phoebe nervously fiddles with the menu in between glances at the restaurant door. She can hardly wait for Claire to arrive. Phoebe has news to share—big news! She imagines Claire's stunned look when she tells her, followed by tons of giggles and hugs.

"Sorry I'm late! Traffic was horrid." Claire says, giving her friend a quick hug before she sits down. She places her book beside her water glass before dropping her purse to the floor.

After a few minutes of placing their orders and catching up, Phoebe takes a deep breath and plunges in: "You won't believe what has happened! Yesterday I—"

She stops and stares in confusion when she sees that Claire has picked up her book and started reading.

Claire looks up and says, "Go on, I'm listening. I just have to check this one thing."

Phoebe, still hesitant, continues, "So yesterday I got a call from Eric—"

"What? That should not have happened!" Claire interjects. Then she looks apologetically at her friend. "Oh, not you. It was something I just read."

As you read through the narrative, what's your reaction? Do you feel Phoebe's excitement draining and disappointment rising? Do you feel Claire is being exceptionally rude to her friend?

Now picture the same scenario, except replace the book with a smartphone. Does that change anything? Well, it certainly makes the situation more common—in fact, an everyday occurrence in our modern world.

Our handy little smartphones let us accomplish so much that they sometimes feel like another appendage. If most Americans check their phone more than a hundred times a day on average, it's not surprising to find that we do so in some "questionable" situations. Consider these statistics from recent surveys:

- 44 percent of smartphone owners have slept with their phone within arm's reach so they can check messages throughout the night,
- 33 percent use their phones during a dinner date,
- 35 percent use their phones while at the movies,
- 19 percent use their phones while in church, and
- 12 percent use their phones while in the shower.[2]

Stress and Unreasonable Expectations

There are several downsides to jumping every time your phone beeps (or you feel a phantom vibration in your pocket). A big one is the stress and pressure of unreasonable expectations.

Because we are now "always connected," we've become a society that expects an immediate response to every text, email, and call. We apply this expectation to ourselves and others, leading us to be constantly checking for a new message that "requires" our attention and feeling impatient when someone doesn't respond quickly and anxious that we won't respond fast enough.

All of this checking and pressure causes stress. The average adult reports feeling a higher stress level than they feel is healthy. On a scale from 1 ("little or no stress") to 10 ("a great deal of stress"), Americans say they are at 4.9

and that 3.6 would be a healthy level.[3] Stress impacts our bodies (for example, physical symptoms such as fatigue, irritability, feeling overwhelmed) and our health habits (sleeping, eating, exercising).

A 2014 study of college students showed a link between cell phone usage and anxiety. Those who used their phone frequently reported feeling tied to it, as if it was just another obligation in their lives, something they had to keep up with.[4] Another study from the United Kingdom estimates that 53 percent of smartphone users suffer from "nomophobia," a fear of being out of mobile phone contact.

Is this just something we have to live with, the price for our high-tech lives? Our opinion is that we don't have to pay that price. We believe it's time to start being a little easier on ourselves and others.

The truth is that most of our phone-checking is unnecessary and that we don't have to bow to the pressure to always be on. To demonstrate this point, consider the table on the next page, which shows all the emails, text messages, and app notifications one of us (Pam) received on a typical Monday:

Type of Notification	Total	Urgency
Emails received	67	No response needed
Emails received	4	Needed a response in 1 or 2 days
Emails received	5	Immediate response needed
Emails sent	20	N/A
Text messages received	6	No response needed
Text messages received	2	Immediate response needed
App notifications	20	No response needed
App notifications	3	Immediate response needed

A quick scan through the numbers shows that most of the "beeps" from my phone were not urgent. So why then am I constantly checking it? Well, as we talked about in chapter 2, our brains crave novelty, and "urgent" messages arrive at just the kind of random schedule that make checking for them a tough habit to break.

Compromising Our Manners

Sometimes, as in the case of Claire and her book in the opening story, responding to every beep and bing from our phone affects our manners. Electronic alerts draw attention away from whatever situation we're in. If we're talking on our phones while checking out at the grocery store, we're not really paying attention to the transaction. The cashier has to fight for our attention to ask a question or take our payment.

If we're texting while in church, we're not really taking in the sermon or fully present in worship. The same applies to playing a game on your phone while attending your child's school concert. Yes, you may stop when your little guy or gal is on stage, but don't all of the performers deserve the same respect and attention?

Also, the sounds and lights from using the phone in public places can disturb others. In a meeting, a cell phone ring disrupts the flow of conversation. In the dark of a movie theater, the light from a high-tech screen distracts the eye.

Finally, how we use our smartphones can degrade our manners by sending the wrong message. Many of us place our phones on the table beside us when we're in a meeting or meeting someone for dinner. By doing so, we're sending a nonverbal message to everyone in the room: "I'm here but available if something better should come along."

That's a painful message when you think about it that way. For most of us, it's probably an unconscious one too, a negative side effect of our high-tech habits.

Missing the Moment

One of the biggest downsides of being too attached to

our devices is missing life moments. As great as the virtual world can be, it falls way short of the real thing, with all of its sights, sounds, smells, tastes, and feelings.

I (Pam) recently traveled to Niagara Falls, Canada, for a conference. I had visited several times before while in high school and remember standing in awe of the majestic beauty, listening to the crashing waters and feeling the mist on my face.

On this visit it was cold and windy, so I opted to go to the IMAX theater instead. They were showing a 4-D movie about Niagara Falls. I wasn't really sure what a 4-D movie was but figured it had to be better than freezing. Well, it had not only the 3-D visual effects, but I experienced the story even more fully with mist falling down, my seat jolting, and the smell of a campfire.

Other than the near heart attack from the seat jolting, it was good to have tried it. However, it remains a pale comparison to my memories of standing on the observation deck with my friends and taking in the real falls.

Each day, God gives us the opportunity to experience big and little moments of life, love, sweetness, joy, peace, and even pain. Sharing those experiences with others and with Him bonds us together. Our high-tech devices can help us to share more with those far away as well. However, we must ensure that we aren't trading virtual moments for real ones.

Smart Tips for Managing Your Smartphone

What do you do if you've developed some bad smartphone habits? Are you doomed to continue responding to every notification, stressed out and missing out on real life? Definitely not! We have some tips for having a healthier relationship with your phone:

- *Establish your own boundaries for when you will check your phone and when you won't.* These may include a designated time of day to check email, messages, and social media.
- *When you are in a public setting such as church, a movie theater, or a restaurant, turn off all notifications.* This includes both the sound and vibration.
- *Put your phone away in situations that require your complete attention.* This includes meetings and face-to-face conversations with loved ones. It may be helpful to picture your phone as the book in our opening story. If you absolutely must put your phone on the table to avoid pocket dialing, make sure it is face down.

- *Get an app to monitor how much time you actually spend on your phone.* Set limits for yourself and stick to them.
- *Practice good manners by giving others your full attention.* This can be hard at times, so remind yourself that whatever notifications you are "missing" right now are most likely not urgent.
- *Savor the moment.* When you feel the urge to check your phone, stop and concentrate on the details in your current situation. What sights, smells, and sounds stand out to you? What are the deeper meanings of the words being spoken?

5

Managing Video Game Habits

*Why Many Guys Are Hooked on Games
(And How to Help Them Play Smart)*

"I was tired and wanted to go to sleep, but my eyes were stuck to the screen. So I kept playing MySims. I was like a moth and it was the flame. Finally, I said "Enough!" I turned it off and went to bed. Then I kept dreaming about it. I don't think I should play that game anymore."

CHARIS, 11

We're so conditioned to sink into our World Gone Bad beliefs and see the vast expanses of the online world as a danger-ous—or, at least, wasteful—place. But as I watch my kids turn to YouTube to sharpen their skills in everything from Minecraft to restringing a lacrosse stick to learning new ukulele chords, I'm thrilled that YouTubers like Stampy exist. And I see signs of God's common grace at work.

CARYN RIVADENEIRA,
"A PARENT'S PRAISE FOR STAMPYLONGHEAD"[1]

The days of Pong and Pac-Man are over. Space Invaders is history. Today's interactive video games are faster, more realistic, and—some people would argue—more addictive.[2]

While video games trace their history back to the 1950s, they've become part of the mainstream culture in only the last two decades. Technological advances have expanded gaming options from consoles, computers, and arcades to social media platforms, mobile devices, and handheld games. Designers have greatly expanded the types of games available, providing entertainment options for everyone, from the ten-year-old boy who wants to kill aliens and save the world to the apartment-dwelling grandmother who relives her childhood by playing Farmville on Facebook.

Chances are you're one of the 53 percent of American adults who plays video games. For young adults and teens, gaming is nearly universal. The video game landscape today differs radically from what most of us grew up with, almost to the point that the term *video games* feels inadequate. For Generation X-ers, the term *video game player* likely prompts the image of a socially awkward teen boy spending hours alone on his computer, blowing up space invaders in between bites of pizza and chugs of Mountain Dew.

An estimated half billion people worldwide spend at least an hour a day playing computer and video games. That's about 3 billion hours a week—with the United States accounting for almost half of those hours. The computer and video game industry now garners an impressive $21 billion, not far behind the movie industry.

Whether you are a gamer yourself or the parent of one,

it's time to learn more about managing video game habits.

The Video Game Landscape

If you're not familiar with today's gaming landscape, it can be a little overwhelming with the variety of platforms/devices and types of games. A brief survey of this landscape will help you get your bearings.

These days video games may be played on stand-alone consoles (such as Nintendo Wii, Sony PlayStation, and Microsoft Xbox), desktop or laptop computers (either online or offline), and handheld devices (Nintendo DS, smartphones). Depending on the capabilities of the device and the type of game, players may play solo, against or with someone else in real time or asynchronously, or with many other players simultaneously, such as in massively multiplayer online games (MMOGs).

With the plethora of games available and new ones being created each day, the industry has yet to establish a standard genre classification. Those who attempt to classify games typically focus more on the game experience—what the player actually does during the game—than the story or setting, as in movies or books. Most games today fall into one of the general categories listed on the next page, although some may be a mix of two or more genres.

Genre	Description
Action	Emphasizes physical challenges, including hand-eye coordination and reaction time
Adventure	Involves puzzle-solving, exploration, and narrative
Party	Allows 2 to 4 players to compete against each other in a board-game-like environment
Puzzle	Requires mental skill as well as dexterity and quick reflexes
Role-Playing	Allows the player to control the actions of the protagonist in a well-defined world
Simulation	Simulates parts of a reality, fictional or real
Shooter	Revolves around shooting, with the play through the eyes of the player character
Sports	Simulates playing a traditional physical sport
Strategy	Requires strategic and/or tactical thinking

Examples
Fruit Ninja, Grand Theft Auto
Skyrim, Super Mario Bros.
Scrabble, Words with Friends
Tetris, Diamond Crush
Final Fantasy, World of Warcraft
Minecraft, Sims
Call of Duty, Halo
Madden Football
Civilization, Endless Space

These general categories are just the beginning of the huge world of video games—a world that can easily overwhelm the uninitiated looking for a birthday gift for her nephew! One more key piece of the video game landscape helps in choosing: the Entertainment Software Rating Board (ESRB) provides ratings for apps and video games that can help consumers make informed choices. The ratings have three components:

- rating categories, which suggest age appropriateness;
- content descriptors, which note why the content has a particular rating or may be of concern; and
- interactive elements, which describe the user's ability to interact, share information, and so on.

The Gamer Experience

Video games represent a modern form of play. Because they come in so many varieties, they open the world of play for many of us who might otherwise think we have outgrown this type of pleasure.

Chapter 2 touched briefly on how interaction with high-tech gadgets activates the pleasure centers in our brains. This applies to the various forms of video games as well. They are fast-paced and often matched to our skill level to provide the right balance between challenge and achievement. Just like many pleasurable activities, they can relieve stress and give us a self-esteem boost when life is dragging us down. Playing with others, whether in person or virtually, helps us feel like we belong and are part of a larger community.

Generally, males are more into video games than their female counterparts. The fact that the content has traditionally focused on sports and combat may explain part of this. Another explanation relates to the nature of video games themselves, with their levels and rewards. As author Kevin Schut points out, "Reality is mundane, completely devoid of swashbuckling and derring-do."[3] In a virtual world, boys go on daring adventures, fighting off pirates, monsters, and space aliens.

We mentioned earlier that it's now estimated that the average American child will spend as much time playing video games as she or he will be in school (from kindergarten to twelfth grade). One nationally representative study of eight- to eighteen-year-olds found that they spent an average of 13.5 hours a week gaming. Among infants to six-year-olds, two out of five had played at least some screen-based games.[4]

For this book we also surveyed 1,013 kids (ages eight

to twelve) from across the country. All attend church monthly and nearly all play video games for at least an hour during a typical week. Similar to what has been reported from other surveys, the kids in our study spent an average of 12½ hours a week playing games, with boys playing for 2 more hours than girls. Although controversy still rages about game addiction, it's notable that 22 percent of boys and 11 percent of girls showed at least three signs of problematic gaming, such as fighting with others over time spent on games, neglecting other activities (for example, chores or schoolwork), and playing games to avoid thinking about real life.

Boundaries and Balance

Do these numbers surprise you? Do they sound like what happens in your own home? We, too, have had to strike a balance between letting our kids enjoy the games they love and making sure they make time for the other areas of their lives. Just a couple of months ago, I (Pam) was having trouble getting my nine-year-old daughter up for church. Our wake-up time during the week is much earlier, so the later Sunday time really shouldn't have been a problem. Then I noticed that our laptop was missing from the dining room. Upon investigating, I discovered that my girl had taken it to her room and was playing

Minecraft late into the night. Our family rule is that the laptop stays out of the bedroom. We had a long talk about how it is fine to enjoy the game, but if it makes her lie or disobey, it may not have a place in her life—and she was getting two screen-free weeks to try it out.

To help keep video game fun in balance, it's important to establish, monitor, and enforce some family rules about when games can be played and for how long, and which games kids can play and websites they can visit. These rules are much easier to monitor and enforce when kids are very young and when the screens are not in their bedrooms.

The "no screens in the bedroom" policy is one recommended by the American Academy of Pediatrics. Among the kids in our study, however, screens (not just one!) in their bedrooms was the norm. Typically these included a computer and a television. Gaming consoles were also particularly common among boys.

Our own study reveals that, compared to kids who do not have screens in their rooms, those that do...

- play video games for more hours a week.
- are more likely to list a Teen or Mature game as one of their favorites.
- are more likely to have three or more signs of problematic gaming.

- tend to avoid difficult or uncomfortable situations more.

Readers should keep in mind that these are simply correlations at this point. We are not saying that allowing the screens in bedrooms causes these behaviors. It's likely that there are complex relationships among all of the factors. However, we do think it's important for parents to be aware of signs that their kids may be playing games more than is healthy or using video games to avoid facing real-life challenges.

One other aspect of video games and game culture must be addressed before we end this chapter: questionable content. Many games contain a great deal of violence or sexuality. Decades of research support a link between consumption of media violence and aggression and violent behavior. The size of the link varies by study. Also, some people are more susceptible to media influence than others, depending on their personality traits and histories.

When managing family video game habits, it's important to stay informed about content. This includes learning about the ESRB ratings and familiarizing yourself with how the games are played. Doing this will also provide you with opportunities to discuss moral topics that may be part of the story line or narrative.

The Truth about Violent Games

Violent video games drew special attention after a series of school shootings. Authorities found that the shooters, almost without exception, were big fans of point-and-shoot games. That sparked debate over the games' ability to fuel real-life hostility. Recent research shows that playing violent games can increase aggressive thoughts, feelings, and behavior. Does that mean every child who plays any kind of game that has violent elements will turn into a cold-blooded killer? Absolutely not. That's unrealistic. But it would be equally foolish to pretend that there's no risk from games that stimulate endorphins, encourage brutality, and then reward violence—a potent combination.

Are violent video games dangerous? Lt. Col. David Grossman, director of the Killology Research Group, is an expert on what it takes to make soldiers more comfortable with taking another life on the battlefield. He sees a parallel with games that put players behind the eyes of the shooter. Just as a flight simulator teaches people to fly a plane, so point-and-shoot games can desensitize us and, in extreme cases, make people more efficient killers. Grossman explains:

> *In Paducah, Ky., a 14-year-old boy brought a .22 caliber pistol to school. He fired eight shots. For the sake of perspective, the FBI says that the average law enforcement officer hits less than one bullet in five in real-world engagement. This young man fired eight shots. He hit eight different students. And we know where he acquired this ability—from video games. His parents had converted a two-car garage into a playroom with video games. He had become a master game player.*
>
> *On that fateful morning, he acted out a set of conditioned responses. He walked in, planted his feet, posted the gun in a two-handed stance, and opened fire. He never moved far to the left or right. He just fired one shot at everything that popped up on his screen. A person's normal response is to shoot at a target until it drops, but video games train you to fire one shot and then move on. And so he proceeded. Most video games give bonus points for head shots. This young man hit five out of eight in that region.[5]*

While few players will take gaming to that extreme, a Christ-follower shouldn't entertain himself or herself with violence in the first place. Even if we'd never actually kill someone, could we be nurturing a love for violence?

Video Game Tips FTW![6]

We live in an exciting time when the video game world is exploding with creativity. The obscure pastime of the few has emerged as a significant part of mainstream culture, particularly among youth. Video games provide hours of entertainment, with some even enhancing some cognitive and spatial skills.

To help your family embrace the good side of video games while avoiding the downsides, we offer these tips:

- *Establish family rules about what games can be played, when, and for how long.* Discuss how video games are a privilege (rather than a right) and what the consequences will be for breaking the rules.
- *Help kids keep games in balance by keeping screens out of the bedroom.* Keep in mind that this decision may be countercultural. Talk about why you are making this choice as a family.
- *Stay up to date on ESRB ratings.* Examine the ratings and descriptions before purchasing a game.
- *Familiarize yourself with the games your kids like to play.* Talk to them about what they like, what they don't, what they are learning, and so on. If you can, spend some time playing with them.

6

Managing Facebook Obsessions

*Why Youth Are Drawn to Social Media
(And How to Keep Them Safe)*

*Here's official proof that the selfie is here to stay—
as of today, if you look up "selfie" in a Merriam-Webster
dictionary, you'll find the following definition: "(n., 2002):
an image of oneself taken by oneself using a digital
camera especially for posting on social networks."*
MADELINE STONE, *BUSINESS INSIDER*

*For you created my inmost being; you knit me together
in my mother's womb. I praise you because I am fearfully
and wonderfully made; your works are wonderful, I know
that full well. My frame was not hidden from you when
I was made in the secret place, when I was woven
together in the depths of the earth.*
PSALM 139:13–15

The desire to use computers to connect socially with others dates back nearly as far as the technology itself. Before MySpace, Facebook, and Twitter changed our culture, people used electronic bulletin boards and chat rooms to socialize.

Today three out of four Internet users belong to a social network site (SNS). Teens and young adults use social media at higher rates than older adults. As teens, boys and girls are equally likely to use social networking sites. However, among adults, women are more involved in SNS than men.[1]

The Draw of Social Media

God has created us as social creatures, designed to connect with each other and with our heavenly Father. Social media allows us to connect with others—sharing words, images, and even videos. At their best, SNS enable us to join others in their stories and bring them into ours. Social media also provides a platform for individuals to share their voice and unite with others who have similar interests and opinions.

As anyone with teens knows, teens' focus lies primarily on their peers. Friendships and being with other teens are supreme. It's only natural then that SNS are a huge draw, allowing youth to stay connected with each other 24/7.

We've touched on some of the downsides of this constant connection in earlier chapters. Let's now consider some specific social media risks and how to manage them.

Risk #1: Talking to strangers

Facebook and many other SNS allow you to create a circle of "friends." Generally it's this circle that will see what you post, and you will see what they share. This is a critical thing to remember each time you accept someone's friend request.

I (Pam) remember the first time I received a Facebook friend request from someone I didn't know. It surprised me, and I spent some time trying to figure out how this person "discovered" my profile. I was raised with a strict warning not to talk to strangers, which made me hesitant to join an SNS in the first place.

For digital natives growing up in the post-Facebook world, connecting with everyone on SNS and sharing everything may seem natural. But our world is fallen. The dangers that our mothers feared when they told us not to talk to strangers are still out there. Moreover, connecting through SNS has the potential for giving details of where kids are and what they are doing to would-be predators.

Risk #2: Sharing to the point of regret

One of those funny e-cards that gets passed around the Internet sums up Risk #2 perfectly:

> *I'm glad Facebook and Twitter were not around when we were young so no one can see all of the stupid things we did.*

The high-tech reality is that once things are shared on the Internet, you never have complete control over where they go and who sees them. Even if you delete a post on your profile, it will always exist somewhere.

That funny post you wrote with your BFF at the mall when you were fifteen may not seem so funny when your twelve-year-old niece finds it eight years later. That passionate picture of you and your current boyfriend will create some awkwardness later if you end up not marrying him.

Being careful about what you share on social media doesn't just have the potential to affect personal relationships. A CareerBuilder survey of hiring managers showed that 37 percent of companies use social media to screen potential candidates. They are looking to see if this possible hire presents himself or herself professionally, is a good fit with the company's culture, and is well rounded. A third of these managers have not hired a candidate because of something they found via social media.[2]

For digital natives, social media has been intricately woven into the fabric of their lives. It is second nature for them to share and post about all they are feeling and experiencing—the good, the bad, and everything in between. Helping them manage their high-tech habits must include teaching them to think carefully about how sharing might affect their relationships now and their future selves.

Risk #3: Curating a false self

At times, maintaining a social media presence can feel like a public performance. We can feel pressured to update our status, send a witty text, or find just the right profile picture. We want to present ourselves in the best light possible, and if we're not careful, we end up with a curated, false virtual look-alike.

Too much attention on maintaining our SNS image carries the risk of narrowing our focus to just "*me.*" The songs "Selfie" by The Chainsmokers and "My Own Little World" by Matthew West depict this self-absorbed tendency. Media headlines have also noted several cross-sectional studies showing higher levels narcissism among young people today, compared to earlier generations.

Curating a social media presence presents another risk as well. A critical development task for teens is answering the question "Who am I?" They explore different roles, styles, and identities—searching for the one that truly represents them. They also often feel that others are as focused on their appearance as they are themselves, that everyone is looking at and evaluating them. Social media may compound this, as others "like," comment on, or ignore their posts.

In a recent survey sponsored by Girl Scouts of the USA, three-fourths of girls said that they feel other girls use SNS "to make themselves look cooler than they are." They also admitted that they purposely downplay some of their own positive characteristics online, such as their intelligence, kindness, and how they try to be a good influence.[3]

Girls with low self-esteem may be especially vulnerable to the stress of social networking and curating their identity. They are more likely to say that their SNS presence doesn't match their true selves. They also report more negative experiences on SNS, such as being bullied or gossiped about.[4]

This consequence of self-curating highlights again the limitations of technology in building relationships. At the end of the day, our SNS profiles and presence are simply a virtual representation of our true selves.

Staying Safe in a #Selfie-Driven World

Social networks and media have opened up wonderful opportunities to connect with old friends and new, both near and far. When managed well, they enhance our sense of community and belonging, strengthen relationships, and give us the chance to encourage and support others. In conclusion, we offer these tips for managing social media:

- *Teach youth about Internet and social media safety.*
- *Set boundaries for who your child can "friend" and what they may share.* This may include requiring that you have access to their profile and activity.
- *Check periodically to find out what your child is experiencing on social media.* Remind them to tell you if someone is bullying them or doing anything else that makes them uncomfortable.
- *Avoid comparisons and remember that your virtual self is not the real you.* We all have ups and downs in life. Some of these get shared on SNS; most do not. If seeing what others post is starting to bring you down, it's time to step back and remind yourself that you're looking through tinted lenses.
- *Maintain a well-rounded offline life.* This includes spending time with family and friends in real life, as well as pursuing hobbies and other interests.

7

Managing the Dark Side of the Web, Part 1

Protecting Our Children from Internet Porn

I have been dealing with pornography (in different ways) since I was a child. . .maybe ten or eleven. When I was younger, there was this photographic magazine my father had that I would look through with no gain. Later I learned to explore my body and found visual aids like lingerie magazines. Later, I would find Internet porn sites. Little by little I found myself in a world filled with different types of attractive visual aids that filled my mind and body with pleasure.

GARY

I am a junior in high school, and things are starting to get difficult. Life is starting to get serious. All these life problems are lurking, and I feel as if I am playing a juggling act in order to keep them at bay. The worst part is the temptations that I'm facing with my girlfriend. See, I was addicted to porn (much like every single one of my classmates and friends) for a long time, and although I am not completely over it, I have done well within the last month. But now my girlfriend is always stressed, and I can't make her happy, and I don't know what to do. So we are starting to do things that I know are not okay. How do I stop? What do I do?

JASON

Judy's son, Hunter, wasn't interested in watching his favorite prime-time TV show or taking on an Xbox video game challenge. After glancing at his watch then muttering something about having a big test to prepare for, the sixteen-year-old excused himself from the dinner table and raced upstairs.

The proud mom smiled at her husband. "And to think—he used to grumble at the thought of doing homework," she said, happy that her grown-up son was behaving so responsibly.

Later that evening, Judy interrupted Hunter's time on the computer with a *tap, tap, tap* on his bedroom door then a friendly reminder: "Shut down and hit the sack."

But when she poked her head into his room, she was stunned by what she saw on the computer screen. Judy turned her head quickly and pretended not to notice. Hunter, on the other hand, scrambled to maintain his cover. He switched off the monitor, flashed a phony smile, and told an outright lie: "Thanks, Mom. Homework's done, and I'm heading to bed."

As Judy pulled shut Hunter's door, her heart began to race and she felt queasy deep in the pit of her stomach. *It can't be true,* she told herself. *Not my son. I must be imagining what I just saw.*

She put her hand back on the doorknob. . .then

paused. *Should I confront him right now? Should I talk to my husband first? Is my boy really living a double life? What on earth are we going to do?*

The sad truth is, what Hunter once used as a tool for learning had lately become a tool of darkness. Internet porn seemed to own him. And with each click of his mouse, the teen was being pulled deeper into an evil web.

Judy had to intervene. . .*fast.* But how?[1]

Does Hunter's struggle hit home? Do you suspect that your own son is compromising his faith? I (Arnie) often tell my constituents that "Satan has a 24/7 strategy to get you to ruin your spiritual life." That statement rings true when we consider the dark side of the web.

In the mid-1990s pornographers recognized the potential of the Internet as a large-scale distribution channel. Two decades later we are reaping the devastating consequences:

- More people visit pornographic websites than Netflix, Amazon, and Twitter combined.[2]
- 12–30 percent of Internet traffic is pornographic.[3]
- One-third of Internet users have experienced unwanted exposure to pornography through pop-up ads, misdirected links, or emails.[4]

- 40–50 percent of young men who attend church regularly admit to viewing pornography at least every few months.[5]

These are just a few of the more reliable statistics. With such an emotionally charged topic, finding reliable information you can trust can be difficult. For example, some sources say the average age of first exposure to pornographic material is ten to eleven years old, while others have that average as young as eight years old. For our purposes, we've only included numbers here to give you some idea of the scope of the problem and to emphasize the importance of protecting your family from the dark side of the web.

Prevention Is Always the Best Cure

As children begin to interact with high-tech gadgets and explore the Internet, it's important to prepare them for the dangers that could lie ahead. Imagine that you are sending your child camping for the first time to a place they have never been before. You would help them pack their backpack, give them some bug spray, show them how to roll their sleeping bag, and so on. You would likely also talk to them about how to stay safe in the woods—for example, stay with the group, don't go swimming alone, watch for tree branches when you're hiking, don't approach wild animals.

Our kids need the same type of preparation before we let them explore the virtual world. This is a continual process, changing as our children develop. In the case of pornography in particular, it also becomes part of educating our children about God's design for sexuality and purity.

Early on, when our kids are very young, the main prevention goal should be to avoid accidental exposure to pornographic material. Thus, we can limit which specific websites they may use and teach them not to click on any link without our permission.

As they mature and begin using the Internet for other purposes, such as researching a school assignment, prevention needs to be stepped up. Now the goal is to prevent both accidental and intentional exposure. A tremendous amount of "information" comes at us (and our kids!) every day. They may hear a word in a song or from a friend and then want to Google it to find out more. With just a few mouse clicks, what started as innocent curiosity can quickly turn to a screen full of images that evoke a surge of emotions and thoughts the child is not ready for.

Filtering and monitoring software that blocks certain

websites and provides a report of activity can be useful. Examples include WebWatcher, Covenant Eyes, and McAfee's Safe Eyes. This type of software is available not just for laptops and desktop computers, but also for smartphones and tablets.

Software alone is not enough. We also need to be talking to our kids, in developmentally appropriate ways, about purity and God's design. As uncomfortable as we may find such conversation, we need to make sure our kids understand that they can come to us with their questions and struggles.

When Prevention Doesn't Work

Even with the best filtering, monitoring, and educating, sometimes kids are exposed to pornography. As upsetting as that is for parents, we must be prepared to help our kids through what can be a traumatic event.

If you learn that your child has seen something sexually explicit, it's important to stay calm and learn more about what happened and how. Ask your child to explain what they saw and how they got to it. Did they click on a familiar website that had been hacked by a pornographer? Did they mistype a website name and end up somewhere they shouldn't be? Did someone send them images or a link to click? Or were they intentionally look-ing for pornography?

Answers to these questions will help you figure out what your next steps are in terms of prevention. Maybe it's time to reiterate Internet safety rules or change some settings on your filtering software. Maybe it's time to have another talk about sexuality and purity.

It's also important to talk to your child about their re-action to what they saw. Depending on the circumstances, they could be feeling grossed out, excited, scared, shocked, or any combination of these. It's important to help them process those feelings and to talk about why you are work-ing to protect them from this dark side.

Raising G-Rated Kids in an X-Rated World

One of the most difficult challenges in our high-tech world is protecting kids from pornography. As long as hu-mans have been creating images, some of those images have been sexually explicit. The hurdles to getting to them, however, were higher—requiring a trip to the local adult store and securing money to purchase them. Today por-nography is just a mouse click away 24/7, often for free.

As upsetting as this reality is, we must remember that we are not powerless. Most of us aren't prepared to cut ourselves completely off from the world and to raise our kids in a protective bubble. Even if we could, those kids would eventually grow up.

Our best choice, then, is to raise kids who are informed and prepared to follow Christ in this fallen world. That includes protecting them from the dark side of the web, using strategies such as these:

- *Teach kids about Internet safety in a way that matches their developmental stage.* When they are younger, you will have more direct control over what they do online. Later you will need to equip them to protect themselves.
- *Keep screens in the "public" part of the house.* Having computers and laptops in a high-traffic area such as the living room or kitchen makes monitoring easier and decreases the chances that kids will be exposed to unwanted images.
- *Consider using filtering and monitoring software.* Talk as a family about why you are using these tools. Check the reports and discuss any problems you find.
- *Talk with your kids about God's design for love, sex, and purity.* Make this an ongoing discussion as

they grow and mature, rather than a one-time "birds and bees" talk.

- *Don't panic if you discover that your child has been exposed to pornography.* Put on your investigator hat and find out how and why it occurred. Help your child to process the experience, and then redouble your prevention efforts.

8

Managing the Dark Side of the Web, Part 2

What to Do When Porn Wrecks Your Marriage

It's been a problem in my marriage for almost eleven years.
The past eight months were the best we have ever had.
I thought he was finally free. He really thought so, too.
I never thought I would actually get to this point. This time
did me in. Overnight I became numb to him. I don't want a
divorce because it would ruin mine and my kids' lives,
so I feel like staying and ruining his.
SPOUSE CONFESSION, XXXCHURCH.COM

Today I start my journey of being porn-free. I have been strug-
gling at this off and on for some time now. Not telling anyone
and hiding it has been very hard on me, and now I am going
to take the stand and be strong for my family. I know that
what I am doing is affecting them, and I need to be better.
HUSBAND CONFESSION, XXXCHURCH.COM

It is for freedom that Christ has set us free.
Stand firm, then, and do not let yourselves
be burdened again by a yoke of slavery.
GALATIANS 5:1

Each year the men's ministry Iron Sharpens Iron holds hundreds of conferences across the country. Men are encouraged and enriched by presentations from top

Christian leaders covering a range of topics from leadership to finances to prayer. Arnie and I (Mike) regularly speak at these conferences, typically on the topic "Managing the Dark Side of Me." Although the talk focuses on temptation in general, we inevitably end up discussing pornography. The rooms are typically packed, and many men open up about their pain and their struggles. They talk about feeling like a slave to lust and porn. They talk about their shame and guilt.

Nearly every one of these guys has a wife and kids. Some are business leaders, respected members of their communities. Some are even pastors, responsible for leading entire congregations. When they are in the grip of pornography, many lives are at risk of being destroyed.

Maybe yours is one of those lives. Maybe your sister's or best friend's is. If so, we've written this chapter for you. We'll start with looking at the physical, spiritual, and relational fallout of porn. Then we'll give you practical strategies for recovery and restoration when porn wrecks your marriage.

Physical Fallout

Pornography addiction has become a common term among researchers and therapists, although psychology has yet to establish an official definition and diagnostic criteria. Because it involves a behavior rather than a substance, and a controversial behavior at that, there's little agreement on whether it's possible to even be addicted. While the scientific community argues over the details, counselors, churches, and ministries are left trying to help hurting families.

Somewhat similar to what we see with other addictive substances, watching pornography activates the pleasure centers of the brain, stimulating the release of dopamine, testosterone, and norepinephrine. In fact, from your brain's perspective, viewing sexual acts on a screen means you are vicariously participating as well. It's getting the body primed for sexual release and etching into memory what stimuli created the arousal. The intensity of pleasure can drive the individual to seek it more or in a more hard-core form to produce the same feelings.

The vast amount of sexually explicit content available, particularly on the Internet, feeds into the brain's craving for novelty. There's always something new or different to see. Although the research evidence is still controversial, logic would then tell us that the more someone views pornography, the more they will want to view it and the harder it will be to stop.

Other physical fallout, with some scientific evidence, relates to sexual performance. A recent study published in an academic journal found that 25 percent of new erectile dysfunction patients are men under forty. This contrasts with just 2 percent fifteen years ago.[1] Heavy pornography use is thought to explain much of this increase, making it more difficult to achieve intimacy with a real partner. Also, the intense imagery and stimulation of sexually explicit materials may retrain your brain to respond only to those types of cues, making real intimacy feel less interesting and exciting. For both of these, anecdotal accounts far outweigh scientific evidence at this point. However, the number of accounts from heavy pornography users and therapists suggest that such consequences are likely.

Spiritual Fallout

In 1 Corinthians 6:18 the apostle Paul writes: *"Flee from sexual immorality. All other sins a person commits are outside the body, but whoever sins sexually, sins against their own body."*

Viewing pornography does indeed affect our spiritual lives. Despite what the media may tell us, it's not an accepted part of the culture, a victimless pastime, or a sign of being sexually free.

Rather, a pornography habit brings with it shame, guilt, isolation, and the need to hide from others. It exerts its own subtle form of slavery, blocking a person from moving closer to Jesus.

In our own Center for Bible Engagement research, we've found that men who view pornography at least once a month struggle frequently (at least a few times a month) with the following:

- hopelessness (46 percent vs. 19 percent)
- bitterness (47 percent vs. 21 percent)
- needing to hide from others (55 percent vs. 20 percent)
- feeling unable to please God (38 percent vs. 21 percent)[2]

Each week families trapped in this struggle write us, asking for prayer. Their requests reveal the spiritual pain they are experiencing:

> *Pray that my wife, Debbie, and I experience breakthroughs in our relationship this year and that our marriage and family remain strong. Also that I*

will continue to be completely free from viewing pornography and habitual masturbation and the associated lustful homosexual and heterosexual thoughts.

I am simply struggling with lust and porn a lot and want to be set free of it so bad, but I can't seem to give it up no matter what I do. Also, I have all these life choices like college and career, and it all scares me, and I am so confused with my life.

Please pray for me. I am struggling spiritually and fighting alcohol and porn addiction. I try to follow Christ but can't seem to stay on the right path. I feel like my prayers are unheard and that God has turned His back on me. I'm a terrible spiritual leader for my family; my family is a mess. My life is a mess, and no matter how I seek Jesus, I can't find peace or change. Why won't God help me?

Although these guys feel trapped by pornography, they may not realize that it's more than just a lustful temptation. Dr. Todd Bowman, a licensed counselor and professor at Indiana Wesleyan University, describes the vicious cycle of compulsive pornography use. It starts with a desire to view pornography and proceeds to acting it out. This is immediately followed by shame, guilt, and the drive to keep it a secret. As the individual's mood worsens and he becomes more isolated, the temptation starts again, as a way to relieve the pain and stress he's feeling.[3]

This can be a powerful cycle, involving long ingrained habits and several brain chemicals. But the good news is that it's not impossible to break.

Relational Fallout

Relationship satisfaction and sexual satisfaction decline when one partner regularly consumes pornography. One experiment found that after several weeks of exposure to nonviolent pornographic videos, college students reported less satisfaction with their partner's physical appearance, sexual performance, affection, and sexual curiosity.

Wives of men involved in pornography experience a tremendous amount of pain and emotional turmoil, similar to those who discover marital infidelity. They may sense that their partners are hiding something, that they feel emotionally distant. When these wives discover the truth, the sense of betrayal pierces their hearts, mixing with anger and rage.

Their self-esteem may suffer a huge blow. The question

"Am I not good enough for you?" crosses their minds as they try to figure out how their husbands got involved in porn in the first place. They may wonder how they can ever "compete" with women who have perfect bodies and are always willing to meet their husband's every need.

At its core, pornography destroys the trust in a marriage. Rebuilding that trust takes a lot of time, commitment, apologizing, forgiveness, support, and accountability. If the discovery occurs after your spouse has developed a strong pornography habit, the road will be even longer, with many ups and downs along the way.

Restoration and Recovery

As painful as the discovery is that your spouse has been viewing pornography, knowing the truth is the first step to recovery. Together you both can fight against this destructive force, and together you will be more powerful to overcome it.

The recovery process begins with confession. This is the time for openness and honesty about what your spouse has been doing, how often, and where. It would be excruciating for both parties to hash through details. However, it's important to share enough so that you can develop an effective relapse prevention plan.

It's also important for the offending spouse to confront the wrong he has done, facing the pain he has caused and seeking forgiveness. You may find it helpful to have this discussion, at least initially, with a neutral third person. Someone such as a pastor or counselor can help keep the conversation from disintegrating into an argument.

Next, develop a relapse prevention plan. Given your specific circumstances, how is your spouse going to avoid falling into pornography again? This plan should include utilizing filtering and monitoring software, removing computers and devices from secluded areas of the house, identifying and removing triggers that usually lead to viewing pornography, and avoiding situations where he's alone with technology.

Several studies (including some of our own) point to the need for accountability. Breaking a pornography habit requires more than just telling yourself, "Stop it!" And trying to stop completely on your own pretty much guarantees failure. This is where an accountability partner comes in.

Look for an accountability partner who is spiritually mature, tough, and also encouraging; someone you can trust completely but who won't be afraid to confront you when you are going into dangerous territory. Your spouse should not be your accountability partner because you will find it too tempting to lie to avoid hurting her.

Because this is a spiritual battle, prayer and Bible engagement must be part of the recovery process as well. Pray with and for each other daily, for healing for your marriage and strength to forgive and overcome. Spend time in God's Word as well, receiving, reflecting on, and responding to what God is saying to you through the Bible.

Healing and rebuilding trust will be an ongoing process. A good marriage or couples therapist can help, especially in the early days when feelings are raw and the pain is most severe.

Finally, utilize the growing number of resources available for families struggling with pornography. The ministry of XXXChurch has a number of excellent resources, including support groups, recovery plans, and monitoring software. Many churches have support groups and resources as well.

9

Engaging Your Spiritual Life

You Can Be High-Tech and Christian

Right now more than one billion people are online,
and what that means to us today is that any Christian
who can log on to a computer can reach one-sixth of the
world's population from their dining room table.
CRAIG VON BUSECK, CBN NEWS

To the weak I became weak, to win the weak.
I have become all things to all people so that
by all possible means I might save some.
1 CORINTHIANS 9:22

Each Sunday our pastor asks us to pull out our Bibles for the day's text. He makes a point of saying, "your Bible you brought from home, an electronic one on your phone, or the one in the pew pocket." With this statement, he's recognizing not only the importance of God's Word in worship, but also the reality that high-tech gadgets can have a place in our spiritual lives.

An early (2004) study by the Pew Internet and American Life Project found that 64 percent of Americans who are online use the Internet for faith-related reasons. This includes searching for information, sharing spiritual or religious materials by email, listening to religious music, sharing or responding to prayer requests, and reading religious or spiritual news.[1] More than a decade later, with the rise of social media, smartphones, tablets, apps, and Internet evangelism, we can only imagine that the use of electronic devices for faith-related purposes has increased.

High-tech gadgets can certainly be a distraction, pulling us away from others and keeping us from spending time with God. But they can also be a tool—opening up new opportunities for growing and sharing our faith.

We asked 163 teens and young adults about how technology affects their spiritual lives. Most talked about both good and bad aspects. High-tech gadgets let you get easily distracted with social media or games, yet they also provide easy access to information. Technology can open the door to temptation or remind you to pray and spend time with God. You can see this tension in the participants' responses:

- On one hand, it allows me to download sermons, use the YouVersion Bible, and get goTandem messages. On the other, social networking distracts from time I should be spending on God.
- It's helpful for me to have apps to aid my Bible study and allow me to research what I'm reading, but it is difficult when I get Facebook notifications

while I'm trying to focus on God.

- I'm able to dig deeper into God's Word anywhere at any time. I can read my Bible app on a plane, on the subway, or on my lunch break. I can even start a group chat and talk about a certain scripture with friends. That's awesome!

- It provides an option for connecting to God on my own time, any time of day (goTandem, Bible reading plans, etc.).

- It helps me understand things better that aren't always explained well in the Bible. I thank God for Google! Don't we all?

Churches and parachurch ministries are also recognizing the power of high-tech gadgets in our lives. Rather than seeing technology as only a competitor for people's time and attention, they're creatively using it for encouragement, teaching, and connecting. Let's explore how.

Internet Evangelism

In today's high-tech world, we turn to Google when we're searching for answers. Searches run the gamut from the mundane to the existential. Those involved in Internet evangelism recognize that someone searching for "How do I find peace?" could be encouraged by the Gospel.

Jesus.net, a global international network of more than fifty Christian organizations and ministries, does just that. They strive to make the Gospel freely accessible on the Internet for every person in the world. They maintain a number of landing pages with titles such as "My life is out of control," using key words that would come up in a Google search. These pages draw the connection between the person's struggle and God or Jesus. As users move through the website, they are directed to a Gospel presentation and given the opportunity to follow Jesus. Other features include discipleship courses and the opportunity to connect with a local church. Their approach is a powerful one—an average of thirty thousand people visit their websites each day.

Other organizations, such as Groundwire, Remedy-Live, and XXXChurch, also use technology to meet people's spiritual needs. The first two offer the opportunity to chat 24/7 with a spiritual coach about what is going on in a person's life. XXXChurch offers information, resources, and support groups for families struggling with pornography and sexual addiction.

In some ways, Internet evangelism ministries take the same philosophical approach as early missionaries who built hospitals and schools. They go to where people are, meet them at their point of pain or need, and then introduce them to the Savior.

Reaching the Most Remote Parts of the World

The Internet's power to reach the world has one serious drawback: 4.4 billion people (primarily in Asia and Africa) do not have access to it. That hasn't stopped some ministries from using technology to share the Gospel.

One example is Good News Production International (GNPI). They provide equipment and basic training to local partners seeking to use Gospel-focused media to reach their communities. One of their innovative programs provides lightweight, portable solar kits for playing media even in areas without electricity.

Faith Comes By Hearing uses audio Bibles to share the New Testament and other portions of scripture with people around the world. In their field programs, small groups gather together to listen to and discuss the Bible. They also have several Bible-based apps, including the Deaf Bible.

Faith-Related Apps

Speaking of apps, did you know that there are several

thousand apps related to faith and Christianity? That number is growing each day. They vary from a simple Bible verse lock screen to podcasts and devotionals that stream content to social networking apps.

YouVersion is hands down the best known. Their free app provides access to 1,092 versions of the Bible in 780 languages. The app includes reading plans that will take you through particular portions of the Bible, much like a traditional devotional.

Many other apps focus on providing devotional and biblical content. In the Conclusion, we'll describe the unique approach we use in our spiritual growth app, goTandem.

OnePlace offers podcasts from leading Christian radio broadcasts. Through this app you can listen to great teaching on your mobile device at a time and place most convenient for you.

For children there's the Superbook Kid's Bible. This app presents the Bible in an engaging, kid-friendly way, including pictures, video, and games.

Other apps focus specifically on connecting a particular Christian community. For example, my (Pam's) local church has one called Planet X that keeps middle schoolers and high schoolers up-to-date on youth group events and activities. Our church is also exploring the possibility of creating a missions or service-focused app that would help congregants plug into service opportunities in our church and our community.

As this very brief survey shows, there's a breathtaking variety of faith-related apps available. We suggest considering your own spiritual needs. How are you doing with hearing from God between Sundays? Do you want a faith-based app for your kids? Are you looking for something that will help you have a richer prayer life? Once you've identified your own goals and needs, explore the options in the app store. You may just find something that will help you connect more with God in this high-tech, busy world!

Virtual Churches

One of the most controversial high-tech initiatives involves virtual churches. In 2007 a handful of churches began experimenting with Internet "campuses." These virtual churches bring worship to any online living room or dorm room.

If you've never experienced an online service, it's a bit hard to describe. It differs from simply streaming a podcast in that virtual churches have scheduled worship times, allowing you to participate simultaneously. Some include chat features or the opportunity to share prayer requests as well. To increase interactivity, they may also have Bible studies or small groups that meet, either online or offline, throughout the week.

Proponents of virtual churches see them as a way to overcome the physical barriers and schedule conflicts that keep people from attending a church. In *SimChurch* Douglas Estes argues that virtual churches reach one of the largest unreached people groups, while traditional churches engage very few of the millions active in the virtual world.[2]

On the other hand, opponents argue that virtual churches can never be real churches. For one, it's impossible to participate in the sacraments online (although some have tried).

A larger argument centers on the biblical ideal of a church as a community of believers. Watching a simulcast and chatting online only go so far and can't replace the strengthening, encouragement, and even messiness that occurs in doing real life together.

It's important to recognize that in-person gatherings are not safe in parts of the world where Christians are persecuted. This may be where virtual churches can serve best.

Recognizing the limitations of technology, most churches have both a physical and virtual presence. The virtual provides seekers a nonthreatening way to begin connecting with a church. It also allows those who occasionally can't attend to still worship during the week. The concern, however, is that some will try to substitute an online experience for real connection and community.

Ultimately only time and research will tell if virtual churches are effective in sharing the Gospel and helping people grow spiritually. We know for now that they represent a creative attempt to minister to a broader group of people who may never cross a church threshold—a trend that may change how churches function in the high-tech world. Chad Hall, director of coaching at Western Seminary, sums the issue up this way:

> *With any new movement, it is wise to ask questions and probe the underlying values, theology, and implications. Even church leaders who are not planning to start an Internet church can benefit from these questions. For example, virtual churches force us to rethink long-held assumptions about what church is, the impact of technology on the soul, and what it really means to participate in a spiritual community.*

The advent of virtual churches may cause many traditional churches to reexamine their own ministry values.[3]

10

Setting Healthy Boundaries

Biblical Solutions for a More Balanced Life

The word of God hidden in the
heart is a stubborn voice to suppress.
BILLY GRAHAM

I always pray with joy. . .being confident of this,
that he who began a good work in you will carry
it on to completion until the day of Christ Jesus.
PHILIPPIANS 1:4, 6

We began this exploration of high-tech habits with a discussion of addiction. Science is still debating whether we can become addicted to smartphones, video games, or even Internet pornography. That debate aside, many of us feel that our high-tech habits have become unbalanced, consuming more of our time and attention than is healthy for our bodies, souls, and relationships.

As we've tackled each subject, we've provided practical tips, tools, and strategies for you and your family. You may find that some work for you, while others do not. At minimum we hope that you will try at least some of them, such as keeping screens out of bedrooms and putting your phone away when talking with someone in real life.

We close with a biblical perspective on having a more

balanced life. We believe that all of life has a spiritual element, and we are called to follow Jesus in every aspect daily. Sometimes it's easy to lose sight of the spiritual or to see the incongruence between scrolling through Facebook at work and being an ambassador for Christ.

That's where general biblical principles come in. Although the words *Facebook* and *smartphone* aren't in any Bible translations, God does have much to say about how we are to live, how we use our time, how we relate to Him, and how we treat each other. Going back to the Bible in this chapter shows us the way forward in setting healthy boundaries in our lives.

The Greatest Commandment

Matthew 22:37–38 records Jesus' response when asked about the greatest commandment: "'Love the Lord your God with all your heart and with all your soul and with all your mind.' This is the first and greatest commandment."

As you look at your own life, where are you following this commandment? Where do you need to make changes? Sometimes we get so focused on the details of life that loving God is no longer the highest priority. We may be doing lots of good things, working hard and serving others. But if we aren't spending time with our Lord, loving and worshipping Him, our life is out of balance.

High-tech gadgets can contribute to this imbalance. Pressure to answer every email and text can keep us from spending time meditating on God's Word. Endless smartphone pings can disrupt our prayers, shifting our attention away from listening to the Holy Spirit.

When you are spending time with God, follow Jesus' model and "disconnect" from the world. You may not be able to go alone to a mountain to pray, but you can turn off your phone or leave it in another room.

You can also literally put God first in your schedule. Speak to Him in prayer before catching up on social media or diving into your favorite video game.

Imagine the scene in Luke 10:38–42 where Jesus visits the home of Mary and Martha. Mary sits at Jesus' feet, listening to his teaching, while her sister scurries to prepare a meal for everyone. When Martha complains about her sister's lack of help, Jesus responds that Mary has chosen "what is better, and it will not be taken away from her" (verse 42).

Now imagine a modern version of that scene. Mary still sits at Jesus' feet, listening with one ear while she posts a Facebook status update that the Great Teacher has come to *her house*.

That's quite a disturbing scene to us. To you, too? This scene can serve as a powerful reminder when our habits keep us from putting God first.

Love Your Neighbor as Yourself

Continuing his teaching on the greatest commandment in Matthew 22, Jesus said, "And the second is like it: 'Love your neighbor as yourself.' All the Law and the Prophets hang on these two commandments" (verses 39–40).

High-tech gadgets can certainly help us to love our neighbors more. We can stay in touch with them over geographic distances, opening opportunities to encourage and pray for one another. On days when they are feeling down, we may remind them that God loves them and so do we.

Knowing that God places such high value on loving others also helps us to manage our high-tech habits. If we're spending so much time playing video games that our spouse has to fight for our attention, we're not loving as we should. If we're letting our cell phones take priority in real-life interactions, we're not showing consideration and care for the person we are with.

Loving others also extends to how we use our words. From behind our high-tech screens, we're tempted to take on another persona, to speak in ways we would never speak face-to-face. It's important to let the second greatest commandment convict our hearts when we're interacting online and offline. Keeping a healthy balance means choosing our words in light of God's standards.

Numbering Our Days

Another biblical principle that helps us keep a healthy balance concerns how we use our time. In Psalm 90:12, Moses asks God to teach us to number our days so that we may gain a heart of wisdom. Each day each of us gets 1,440 minutes. That's a finite number—we can't add to it, though some days we wish we could!

An important part of a balanced life is looking carefully at how we spend our time. How much have we allotted to each area of our lives—family, work, exercise, sleep, service, relaxation, and so on? In which areas do we feel time-pressed, as if we never have enough? Which activities are taking up too much of our time and need to be scaled back?

Keeping the principle of numbering our days in mind is especially important in the area of high-tech habits.

So much of what we do on our gadgets, from games to watching movies to searching for information, can easily become a huge time black hole if we let it. To achieve a healthier balance, we must be disciplined, setting limits for ourselves on how much time we'll devote to each area.

The Temple of the Holy Spirit

Although people often think of the Bible mainly for its spiritual guidance, it also has much to say about how we treat and care for our physical bodies. For example, the apostle Paul reminded the Corinthian believers that their bodies are temples of the Holy Spirit (1 Corinthians 6:19).

How can the biblical principle of respecting your body as the Spirit's dwelling place and God's creation help you lead a more balanced life? First, it can be an encouragement to make healthy choices when it comes to diet, exercise, and proper rest. Our high-tech gadgets are very good at many things, though getting us moving is not usually one of them. For many of us, then, this principle convicts us to put our devices down more often and get moving. For others this means turning off the screens earlier at night to ensure a good night's sleep.

A second way understanding God's view of our bodies

helps is by strengthening our resolve to avoid the dark side of the web. We're called to live according to God's standards for sexual purity. Pornography and its common consequences have no place in that temple.

And Whatever You Do in Word or Deed

Our last biblical principle encompasses all aspects of a balanced life in our high-tech world. Turning again to one of Paul's epistles, we read: "Whatever you do, whether in word or deed, do it all in the name of the Lord Jesus, giving thanks to God the Father through him" (Colossians 3:17; see also 1 Corinthians 10).

Modern technology—whether smartphones or tablets or social media or video games—are tools created by humans. At their core they are neutral. It's how we use them that determines whether they lead us closer to Jesus or further away. That's why this verse from Colossians is so powerful! Whenever we're feeling overwhelmed, overtaxed, and out of balance, it's time to take a step back and reevaluate. Are we doing all to the glory of God?

This teaching applies to both the big and little details of our lives. It definitely includes avoiding sin and those things that lead us away from God. It also includes the positive things, the ones that God is calling us to do. That could include sharing a kind word with the cashier in the grocery checkout line or staying focused on work when we'd rather be playing Candy Crush.

Keeping our focus on Jesus means staying engaged in all aspects of our lives. There's room for high-tech gadgets, as long as we don't let them crowd out the other things that are part of this rich, wonderful creation God has given us. Most of all, we must have the discipline to manage our habits so that loving God, following Him, and living out His purpose are our main priorities.

Conclusion:
A Journey in Tandem

*Finally, a Positive App with
the Right Connection—God!*

When my phone chimes from the goTandem app and my husband says, "Who's texting you?" I always say "God is texting me." It has opened up many opportunities and conversations where they would not necessarily have been.

GT USER

For everything that was written in the past was written to teach us, so that through the endurance taught in the Scriptures and the encouragement they provide we might have hope.

ROMANS 15:4

In the beginning of this book, we talked about how technology and media play huge roles in our ministry. Seventy-six years ago, the founder of Back to the Bible, Theodore Epp, wanted to use the cutting-edge technology of his day to share God's Word around the world. This approach has been part of our DNA since.

We've spent the past decade researching the lives of more than 150,000 people. We discovered that in the busyness of everyday life, our relationship with God often gets neglected. But it doesn't have to be that way. That's why we created goTandem—a free daily spiritual growth app. Whether you are someone just exploring the claims of the Bible, a new Christian, or someone who has been a follower for decades, you can connect with God each day.

Bible Engagement: A Key Ingredient for a Healthy Spiritual Life

Bible engagement occurs when we receive what the Bible says, reflect on its meaning, and respond accordingly with our actions. Through our research, we've learned that the Bible has the biggest impact on our lives—in overcoming temptation, building healthier relationships, and providing hope in uncertainty—when we begin considering bits of scripture throughout the day at least four days a week. More is better. Less is significantly worse.

When we asked people what keeps them from spending time with God, they almost universally said, "I'm too busy." Most of us live at a frenetic pace. Between commuting, work, kids' activities, church, and household chores, there's little room left in the day to sit quietly before our Lord.

Hearing what God says in His Word four days a week, then, might seem like a lot, but with goTandem, it's manageable. Providing a personalized experience with the Bible, goTandem delivers meaningful content directly to you exactly when you need it. Your journey begins with a few short questions about where you are spiritually. The built-in logic then matches you with our entire content library, delivering to you pieces that most closely match your strengths and needs.

More Than Just Another Devotional

Daily devotionals remain some of the most popular books on the market today. Some focus on a particular topic (for example, the goTandem titles *Growing in Christ: 40 Days to a Deeper Faith* and *Overcoming the Hurt: 60 Thoughts on Life's Temptations, Trials, and Triumphs*), while others are a collection of different reflections on particular Bible passages. But goTandem is more than a devotional. It's different because the customized biblical content you receive is based on your unique spiritual needs. The messages you get today will be different than what your spouse or best friend receives.

Another difference is that the content is primarily straight scripture. We want to help you hear clearly what God is saying to you at this moment, without our words or voices getting in the way.

Unlike a typical devotional, your goTandem content comes in a variety of forms. One message may be a short section of scripture, often with a question or two to help you reflect on God's message. Some are one- to three-minute video or audio pieces. Whatever the form, each message is designed to help strengthen and encourage you by taking an honest look at what the Bible says and how applying it moves you closer to Christ.

Would you like to go into a topic deeper? No problem. We have options for that, too. You can click on the verses in any message to open the full chapter in an online Bible. Each message has a Notes section where you can add your own thoughts.

We also have a track feature where you can explore topics such as the following:

- forgiveness
- joy
- worry
- the Gospel of Mark (audio)
- through the Bible
- What does the Bible say about. . . ?
- when life hurts

You May Now Use Your Portable Electronic Devices

We're excited about the possibilities that God is opening up in using technology for ministry. If the average adult looks at their smartphone more than a hundred times a day, that's a hundred chances to connect with God or share with others.

We could go on and on about goTandem. But instead of doing that, we have a three-minute video that does a great job of telling the story. We invite you to go to goTandem.com/resources to watch the video.

We would also love for you to download goTandem and try it out for yourself. It's available in Google Play and the App Store. We look forward to being your daily spiritual growth companion.

Notes

Introduction: Are We Connected . . . or Addicted?

1. "Mobile Technology Fact Sheet," Pew Research Center, January 2014, http://www.pewinternet.org/fact-sheets/mobile-technology-fact-sheet/.

2. Dr. Archibald D. Hart and Dr. Sylvia Hart Frejd, *The Digital Invasion: How Technology Is Shaping You and Your Relationships* (Grand Rapids: Baker, 2013), 27.

3. Joanna Moorhead, "Why We Shouldn't Worry about Teenagers Using Mobile Phones," *The Guardian*, May 20, 2014, http://www.theguardian.com/commentis-free/2014/may/20/teenagers-mobile-phones-study-smartphone-use-addictive.

1. Hashtag Help: Cluing In to Our Electronic Addictions

1. Snejana Farberov, "Parents Were So Immersed in Fantasy Video Game World Where Their Avatars Married and Had Jobs, They Let Real-Life Daughter, 2, Nearly Starve to Death." *DailyMail*, October 11, 2013, http://www.dailymail.co.uk/news/article-2455567/Parents-immersed-video-game-daughter-nearly-starved-death.html#ixzz3O4UDQR84.

2. Kevin Holesh, "I'm Addicted to My iPhone," June 26, 2014, https://medium.com/@kevinholesh/im-addicted-to-my-iphone-4b9601e2776f.

3. Elise Hu, *New Numbers Back Up Our Obsession with Phones*, National Public Radio, October 10, 2013, http://www.npr.org/blogs/alltechconsidered/2013/10/09/230867952/new-numbers-back-up-our-obsession-with-phones; KPCB (Kleiner, Perkins, Caufield, Byers), *Internet Trends Report 2014*, May 28, 2014, http://www.kpcb.com/internet-trends.

4. Amanda Lenhart, "Cell Phones and American Adults," Pew Research Center, September 2, 2010, http://www.pewinternet.org/2010/09/02/cell-phones-and-american-adults/.

5. Harris Interactive, *2013 Mobile Consumer Habits Study*, 2013, http://pages.jumio.com/rs/jumio/images/Jumio Mobile Consumer Habits Study-2.pdf.

6. Jane McGonigal, "Gaming Can Make a Better World," TED Talks, March 2010, http://www.ted.com/talks/jane_mcgonigal_gaming_can_make_a_better_world/transcript?language=en.

7. Andrew Kalinchuk, "Chat Apps to Double SMS Text Messaging by End of 2013," *Digital Trends*, April 29, 2013, http://www.digitaltrends.com/mobile/chat-apps-to-double-sms-traffic-by-end-of-2013/.

8. Amanda Lenhart, "Teens, Smartphones and Texting," Pew Research Center, March 19, 2012, http://www.pewinternet.org/2012/03/19/teen-smart-phones-texting/.

9. *The Social Habit 2014*, Edison Research, 2014, http://www.edisonresearch.com/wp-content/up-loads/2014/07/the-social-habit-2014.pdf.

10. Tony Dokoupil, "Is the Internet Making Us Crazy? What the New Research Says," *Newsweek*, July 9, 2012.

11. Ibid.

12. Mary A. Fischer, "Manic Nation: Dr. Peter Whybrow Says We're Addicted to Stress," *The Pacific Standard*, June 19, 2012.

13. Greg Beato, "Internet Addiction: What Once Was Parody May Soon Be Diagnosis,". *Reason*, August–September 2010, http://reason.org/news/show/internet-addiction-diagnosis.

14. American Psychological Association, "Internet Gaming Disorder Fact Sheet," *Diagnostic and Statistical Manual of Mental Disorders*, 5th ed., May 2013.

15. American Society of Addiction Medicine, *Public Policy Statement: Definition of Addiction*, January 2010; http://www.asam.org/for-the-public/definition-of-addiction.

16. A. Weinstein and M. Lejoyeux, "Internet Addiction or Excessive Internet Use," *American Journal of Drug and Alcohol Abuse*, August 2010, 277–83.

17. Justin McCurry, "Internet Addiction Driving South Koreans into Realms of Fantasy," *The Guardian*, July 13, 2010.

2. What Happens in Our Brains

1. Benjamin Carson, "Dr. Ben Carson Extended

Interview," January 11, 2008, http://www.pbs.org/wnet/religionandethics/2008/01/11/january-11-2008-dr-ben-carson-extended-interview/4847/.

2. Gary W. Small, Teena D. Moody, Prabha Siddarth, Susan W. Bookheimer, "Your Brain on Google: Patterns of Cerebral Activation during Internet Searching," *American Journal of Geriatric Psychiatry*, February 2009, 116–26.

3. M. J. Koepp, R. N. Gunn, A. D. Lawrence, V. J. Cunningham, A. Dagher, T. Jones, D. J. Brooks, C. J. Bench, P.M. Grasby, "Evidence for Striatal Dopamine Release during a Video Game," *Nature* 393 (May 21, 1998): 266–68, D. H. Han, Y. S. Lee, K. C. Yang, E. Y. Kim, I. K. Lyoo, P. F. Renshaw, "Dopamine Genes and Reward Dependence in Adolescents with Excessive Internet Video Game Play," *Journal of Addiction Medicine* 1, no. 3 (September 2007): 133–38.

4. D. A. Fair, B. L. Schlaggar, A. L. Cohen, F. M. Miezin, N. U. Dosenbach, K. K. Wenger, M. D. Fox, A. Z. Snyder, M. E. Raichle, S. E. Petersen, "A Method for Using Blocked and Event-Related fMRI Data to

Study 'Resting State' Functional Connectivity," *Neuro-Image* 35, no. 1 (March 2007): 396–405, M. E. Raichle, A. Z. Snyder, "A Default Mode of Brain Function: A Brief History of an Evolving Idea," *NeuroImage* 37, no. 4 (October 1, 2007): 1083–90, B. R. White, A. Z. Snyder, A. L. Cohen, S. E. Petersen, M. E. Raichle, B. L. Schlaggar, J. P. Culver, "Resting-State Functional Connectivity in the Human Brain Revealed with Diffuse Optical Tomography," *NeuroImage* 47, no. 1 (August 1, 2009): 148–56.

5.   Timothy D. Wilson, David A. Reinhard, Erin C. Westgate, Daniel T. Gilbert, Nicole Ellerbeck, Cheryl Hahn, Casey L. Brown, Adi Shaked, "Just Think: The Challenges of the Disengaged Mind," *Science*, July 4, 2014, 75–77.

6.   Michio Kaku, *The Future of the Mind: The Scientific Quest to Understand, Enhance, and Empower the Mind.* (New York: Anchor, 2015), 4.

7.   Eyal Ophif, Clifford Nass, and Anthony Wanger, "Cognitive Control in Media Multitaskers," *Proceedings of the National Academy of Sciences of the United States of*

America, September 15, 2009, http://www.ncbi.nlm.nih.gov/pmc/articles/PMC2747164/.

8.   B. Wood, M. S. Rea, B. Plitnick, and M. G. Figueiro, "Light Level and Duration of Exposure Determine the Impact of Self-Luminous Tablets on Melatonin Suppression," *Applied Ergonomics* 44, no. 2 (March 2013): 237–40; M. G. Figueiro, B. Wood, B. Plitnick; and M. S. Rea (2011), "The Impact of Light from Computer Monitors on Melatonin Levels in College Students," *Neuro Endocrinology Letters* 32, no. 2 (2011): 158–63.

9.   "Insufficient Sleep Is a Public Health Epidemic," Centers for Disease Control, January 13, 2014, http://www.cdc.gov/features/dssleep/.

10. In urban vernacular, "vamping" also has another, unrelated sexual meaning.

3. Virtual vs. Real Relationships

1.   Sherry Turkle, *Alone Together: Why We Expect More from Technology and Less from Each Other* (New York: Basic Books, 2012), 11.

2.   Ibid.

3.   Gretchen Anderson, "Loneliness among Older Adults: A National Survey Adults 45+," *AARP*, September 2010, http://www.aarp.org/personal-growth/transitions/info-09-2010/loneliness_2010.html.

4.   Yoram Bachrach, Michal Kosinski, Thore Graepel, Pushmeet Kohli, and David Stillwell, "Personality and Patterns of Facebook Usage," Web Science '12 Conference, June 22–24, 2012, Evanston, IL, http://research.microsoft.com/en-us/um/people/pkohli/papers/bkgks_acmwebsci_2012.pdf.

5.   Moira Burke, Cameron Marlow, and Thomas Lento, "Social Network Activity and Social Well-Being," Proceedings of the SIGCHI Conference on Human Factors in Computing Systems, April 10, 2010, http://www.cameronmarlow.com/media/burke-2010-social-well-being.pdf.

6.   In the case of physical abuse, threats, or stalking, electronic communication may not be safe either, because many contain location tags and other identifiable information. We recommend seeking the help of a trained family violence or law enforcement specialist in these cases.

7.   Maeve Duggan, "Online Harassment," Pew Research Center, October 22, 2014, http://www.pewinternet.org/author/mduggan/.

8.   Brendan L. Smith, "Are Internet Affairs Different?" *American Psychological Association Monitor* 42 (March 2011): 48.

4. Managing Our Addiction to Devices

1.   Gerald G. May, MD, *Addiction and Grace* (San Francisco: HarperCollins, 1988), 3–4.

2.   Harris Interactive, *2013 Mobile Consumer Habits Study,* http://pages.jumio.com/rs/jumio/images/Jumio Mobile Consumer Habits Study-2.pdf; "Mobile Technology Fact Sheet," Pew Research Center, January 2014, http://www.pewInternet.org/fact-sheets/mobile-technology-fact-sheet/.

3.   "Stress in America," *American Psychological Association*, 2009, https://www.apa.org/news/press/releases/stress/2009/stress-exec-summary.pdf

4.   Andrew Lepp, Jacob E. Barkley, and Aryn C.

Karpinski, "The Relationship between Cell Phone Use, Academic Performance, Anxiety, and Satisfaction with Life in College Students," *Computers in Human Behavior*, February 2014, 343–50.

5. Managing Video Game Habits

1.   Caryn Rivadeneira, "A Parent's Praise for Stampylonghead," *Think Christian*, September 2, 2014, http://thinkchristian.reframemedia.com/a-parents-praise-for-stampylonghead.

2.   Michael Ross, *BOOM: A Guy's Guide to Growing Up* (Wheaton, IL: Tyndale House, 2003), 176.

3.   Kevin Schut, *Of Games and God: A Christian Exploration of Video Games* (Grand Rapids: Brazos, 2013), 1.

4.   Douglas Gentile, "Pathological Video-Game Use among Youth Ages 8 to 18: A National Study," *Psychological Science*, 2009, 594–602.

5.   David Grossman, quoted in Ross, *BOOM*, 176–77.

6.   FTW! is gamer lingo meaning "For the win!"

6. Managing Facebook Obsessions

1. Kimberlee Salmond and Kristen Purcell, "Trends in Teen Communication and Social Media Use: What's Really Going on Here?" February 9, 2011, http://www.girlscouts.org/research/publications/stem/pew_internet_girl_scout_webinar.pdf2.

2. "Number of Employers Passing on Applicants Due to Social Media Posts," CareerBuilder.com, June 26, 2014, http://www.careerbuilder.com/share/aboutus/pressreleasesdetail.aspx?sd=6%2F26%2F2014&id=pr829&ed=12%2F31%2F2014.

3. Salmond and Purcell, "Trends in Teen Communication and Social Media Use."

4. Ibid.

7. Managing the Dark Side of the Web, Part 1

1. Adapted from Michael Ross and Susie Shellenberger, *What Your Son Isn't Telling You: Unlocking the Secret World of Teen Boys* (Minneapolis: Bethany House, 2010), 105–6.

2. "Porn Sites Get More Visitors Each Month

Than Netflix, Amazon and Twitter Combined," *Huffington Post*, May 4, 2013, http://www.huffingtonpost.com/2013/05/03/internet-porn-stats_n_3187682.html.

3. Ibid.

4. J. Wolak, K. Mitchell, and D. Finkelhor, *Online Victimization: 5 Years Later*, National Center for Missing and Exploited Children, 2006, www.unh.edu/ccrc/pdf/CV138.pdf, Publication 07-06-025.

5. Arnie Cole and Pamela Caudill Ovwigho, *Christian Men and the Temptation of Pornography*, Center for Bible Engagement, October 2010, http://www.centerforbibleengagement.org/images/stories/pdf/Christian_Men_and_Pornography_Oct_2010.pdf.

8. Managing the Dark Side of the Web, Part 2
1. A. Mialon, A. Berchtold, P. A. Michaud, G. Gmel, and J. C. Suris, "Sexual Dysfunctions among Young Men: Prevalence and Associated Factors," *Journal of Adolescent Health* 51, no. 1 (July 2012): 25–31.
2. Arnie Cole and Pamela Caudill Ovwigho, *Christian Men and the Temptation of Pornography*, Center for

Bible Engagement, October 2010, http://www.center-forbibleengagement.org/images/stories/pdf/Christian_Men_and_Pornography_Oct_2010.pdf.

3. Todd Bowman, *Introduction to Sexual Addiction Treatment*, freedomfiveone.com, accessed February 13, 2015, through moodle. Cf. Covenant Eyes, http://www.covenanteyes.com/science-of-porn-addiction-ebook/.

9. Engaging Your Spiritual Life

1. Stewart M. Hoover, Lynn Schofield Clark, Lee Rainie, "Faith Online: 64% of Wired Americans Have Used the Internet for Spiritual or Religious Purposes," Pew Internet and American Life Project, April 7, 2004, http://www.pewinternet.org/files/old-media/Files/Reports/2004/PIP_Faith_Online_2004.pdf.pdf.

2. Douglas Estes, *SimChurch: Being the Church in the Virtual World* (Grand Rapids: Zondervan), 2009.

3. Chad Hall, "Church. . .Virtually," *Leadership Journal*, Fall 2009.

NOTES

NOTES

NOTES

NOTES

NOTES